AI for Qualitative Research

Diana Garcia Quevedo · Josue Kuri

AI for Qualitative Research

A Hands-On Guide for Management Scholars

Diana Garcia Quevedo
Center of Research in Sustainability
(RESET)
ESCP Business School
Paris, France

Josue Kuri
Principal Scientist
San Francisco, CA, USA

ISBN 978-3-032-08871-0   ISBN 978-3-032-08872-7   (eBook)
https://doi.org/10.1007/978-3-032-08872-7

This work was supported by Josue Kuri.

Cover illustration: © Melisa Hasan

This Palgrave Macmillan imprint is published by the registered company Springer Nature Switzerland AG
The registered company address is: Gewerbestrasse 11, 6330 Cham, Switzerland

If disposing of this product, please recycle the paper.

Competing Interests The authors have no competing interests to declare that are relevant to the content of this manuscript.

CONTENTS

LIST OF FIGURES

CHAPTER 1

Introduction

Abstract This chapter explains the book's objective, its structure, and additional resources provided within. It emphasizes the importance of understanding the technology underlying large language models to leverage their capabilities effectively.

Keywords Qualitative analysis · Qualitative research · Large language models

Traditionally, qualitative researchers have manually analyzed textual data, such as interviews, field notes, and archival documents, to uncover patterns and generate rich, context-sensitive understandings of the human experience (Dana & Dumez, 2015; Grodal et al., 2021). Today, we stand at the intersection of tradition and innovation. The advent of large language models (LLMs), such as OpenAI GPT models and Google Gemini models, heralds a transformative era for qualitative research by offering new tools that can process vast amounts of data with remarkable speed and efficiency.

This book is designed as a practical guide for researchers eagerly integrating LLM-based algorithms into their qualitative work. We aim to equip you with the basic technical know-how and critical insights necessary to harness these models effectively while remaining mindful of their limitations. As you will discover throughout the book, there are

1

practical advantages when implementing LLMs through programming applications. Coding facilitates data handling, increases control over LLM parameters, helps manage LLM limitations, and allows the combination of multiple models and techniques, improving data processing and analysis.

We advocate for a foundational understanding of LLM technology, empowering researchers to become *educated users* able to leverage AI capabilities effectively and ethically. As such, this book provides explanations of the underlying technology, including LLMs' limitations, as well as considerations when employing them in research projects.

To facilitate hands-on learning and practical application of LLMs, this book provides a custom-designed dataset and sample code in a dedicated GitHub repository named Diana-GQ/ai_for_qualitative_analysis (https://github.com/Diana-GQ/ai_for_qualitative_analysis). GitHub is a web-based platform for sharing code and collaborating on development projects.

For ethical considerations and data protection, we created a dataset of 1,115 synthetic social media posts representing ten imaginary personas. This dataset is exclusively for educational purposes, allowing you to practice and explore LLM applications in qualitative analysis without the risks associated with real-world private or proprietary data. The dataset can be downloaded and used as input to the code examples provided in the repository. While the data and code are freely available for educational use, they are protected by the same copyright agreement as the rest of the book and are not intended for commercial use.

Although the book is written for noncoders, it requires a learning effort to acquire basic programming skills. For true beginners, we provide links to external resources where you can complement the knowledge we provide in this book. We recognize that implementing coding for the first time represents a major challenge. However, we believe that this is a worthy investment that enables you to take full advantage of the constantly expanding capabilities of LLMs. While the book's intent is not to teach coding, we believe that this skill is critical for researchers to realize the full potential of emerging AI technologies. We encourage you to use all the resources provided with this book and experiment with the code scripts provided.

To facilitate its use as a hands-on guide, the book is divided into two parts. The first part provides foundational knowledge of LLM technology, along with its application for management research and the associated ethical considerations. The second part provides concrete examples of how to use LLMs in qualitative analysis.

Part 1 includes Chapters 2 to 4. It covers the basic knowledge needed when leveraging LLMs for qualitative analysis in management research. Chapter 2 provides a brief history of the origins of LLMs, their technology, and their limitations. Chapter 3 provides a literature review on the use of natural language processing (NLP) and LLMs in management research. Chapter 4 touches on the main ethical considerations when deploying research projects using LLMs as analytical tools.

Part 2 includes Chapters 5 to 11. It involves coding examples and explanations to leverage LLMs for qualitative analysis. Part 2 explains and expands upon the method developed by Garcia Quevedo, Glaser, and Verzat in "Enhancing Theorization Using Artificial Intelligence: Leveraging Large Language Models for Qualitative Analysis of Online Data" (2025).

Chapter 5 aims to familiarize noncoders with basic coding functions, enabling them to understand the coding logic, and introduces the systems and tools for using NLP and LLMs. Chapter 6 delves into the use of LLMs in qualitative analysis, following the method proposed by Garcia Quevedo et al. (2025). This method enhances qualitative inductive analysis by leveraging LLMs to efficiently select the most relevant data and gain deep insights from large datasets, preparing the groundwork for manual inductive analysis. It combines different NLP tasks via traditional and LLM-based models. Chapters 7 to 10 explain each of these tasks, providing the code and recommendations to implement them.

Chapter 7 introduces basic data exploration techniques. Chapter 8 expands on the use of LLMs for classification. Chapter 9 delves into the use of LLMs for topic modeling, a specialized form of clustering. Chapter 10 explains information retrieval and retrieval-augmented generation (RAG) as a useful generative technique for retrieving and synthesizing information. The last chapter, Chapter 11, explores the expanded possibilities of LLMs, which are constantly evolving.

We hope that the following pages will provide you with the necessary knowledge and tools to strengthen your analytical skills and scope through the effective and responsible use of LLMs. Our goal is to empower researchers to leverage LLMs, increasing their analytical capabilities and enhancing their ability to generate comprehensive and insightful qualitative studies.

References

Dana, L. P., & Dumez, H. (2015). Qualitative research revisited: Epistemology of a comprehensive approach. *International Journal of Entrepreneurship and Small Business*, 26(2), 154–170. https://doi.org/10.1504/IJESB.2015.071822

Garcia Quevedo, D., Glaser, A., & Verzat, C. (2025). Enhancing theorization using artificial intelligence: Leveraging large language models for qualitative analysis of online data. *Organizational Research Methods*, 29(1), 92–112. https://doi.org/10.1177/10944281251339144

Grodal, S., Anteby, M., & Holm, A. L. (2021). Achieving rigor in qualitative analysis: The role of active categorization in theory building. *Academy of Management Review*, 46(3), 591–612. https://doi.org/10.5465/amr.2018.0482

Part I

Overview of Artificial Intelligence, Machine Learning, Natural Language Processing, and Large Language Models

Abstract This chapter provides an overview of the technology underpinning large language models (LLMs). It introduces the historical context of artificial intelligence (AI), from symbolic systems to statistical approaches and deep neural networks, highlighting milestones in natural language processing (NLP). It also addresses the limitations of LLMs, such as hallucinations, biases, and a lack of explainability, and the different types of LLMs according to their information-sharing approaches. The chapter aims to help readers understand LLMs and their underlying algorithms, setting the stage for a deeper exploration of ethical considerations and applications in subsequent sections of the book.

Keywords Artificial intelligence · Natural language processing · Large language models

Before addressing the main topic of the book, this chapter introduces artificial intelligence (AI), machine learning (ML), natural language processing (NLP), and large language models (LLMs). This chapter offers a historical perspective on AI with a focus on natural language processing, which has influenced the development of AI from early systems for language translation and speech recognition to present-day applications such as chatbots, agents, and other systems based on LLMs.

© The Author(s) 2026
D. Garcia Quevedo and J. Kuri, *AI for Qualitative Research*,
https://doi.org/10.1007/978-3-032-08872-7_2

The chapter aims to help you understand LLMs and their underlying algorithms before integrating them into a research project. This understanding is important for making informed decisions about when and how to use the models and for encouraging careful use of their outputs rather than unquestioningly trusting them.

NATURAL LANGUAGE PROCESSING

NLP is a subfield of artificial intelligence focused on enabling computers to process, analyze, and generate human language, both text and speech, in a meaningful way. NLP tasks vary widely, from simple tasks such as part-of-speech (POS) tagging, which assigns grammatical labels to words (noun, verb, etc.), to more complex tasks such as semantic analysis, which seeks to understand the meaning of words, sentences, and larger texts. Other important NLP tasks include analyzing the grammatical structure of sentences through syntactic parsing, identifying and classifying entities such as names and locations with named entity recognition (NER), and determining the emotional tone of a text via sentiment analysis. Other analytical tasks involve measuring how close two sentences are in meaning, known as sentence similarity, and identifying underlying themes in collections of documents through topic modeling. NLP also focuses on creating or transforming language, such as with machine translation to convert text between languages, text summarization to create concise summaries from longer documents, and text generation to produce coherent, human-like text. Finally, speech processing is another key area that handles the conversion of speech to text and text back to speech.

NLP tasks are embedded in systems and applications that we use every day. For example, customer support systems use chatbots and virtual assistants to handle queries, search engines rely on NLP to improve search relevance and answer user questions, and multilingual services employ machine translation. NLP also plays a critical role in content moderation by detecting inappropriate or harmful content on online platforms. NLP is applied in specialized fields, such as healthcare to analyze medical records, marketing to gauge customer opinions, education for automated grading, legal and compliance for document analysis, and finance for market insights. NLP is also used in creative functions, with tools that assist in drafting articles, stories, and poetry. The ongoing development of NLP enabled by LLMs continues to expand the range of its applications.

A Brief History of AI and NLP

The AI journey began in the 1950s with symbolic systems and formal logic, where researchers attempted to mimic human reasoning via structured rules. These approaches rely on the idea that human reasoning can be distilled into a series of logical steps, where symbols represent concepts or objects and rules define the relationships and operations between them. For example, "if–then" statements enabled machines to draw conclusions from premises, such as deducing that "all humans are mortal" and "Socrates is human" imply that "Socrates is mortal." While these methods laid a solid foundation, their reliance on explicitly defined rules and logic made it difficult to address the complexity of human language and thought.

By the late 1970s and early 1980s, statistical approaches that relied on probability concepts rather than rules had become increasingly common, offering a more flexible framework for addressing real-world situations. Bayesian models, for instance, address uncertainty by combining prior knowledge with new available information (Bolstad & Curran, 2017). Developments in this space, such as Bayesian networks (Peal, 1985), provide a practical way to represent probabilistic relationships among variables and to reason about causal relationships. The applications of Bayesian models include spam filtering, recommendation systems, fraud detection, assessment of credit risk, medical diagnosis, disease prediction, and clinical decision-making (Green et al., 2022). Hidden Markov models (HMMs) are another type of statistical model used to represent systems that transition between states that cannot be directly measured (Rabiner, 1989). For example, HMMs are used in ecology studies to characterize the behavioral states of wild animals (sleeping, eating, etc.) from location and speed measurements obtained from GPS collars (McClintock & Michelot, 2018). HMMs have also been used in NLP applications such as speech-to-text conversion and part-of-speech (POS) tagging.

In addition to statistical methods, the 1980s saw the revival of neural networks, a type of machine learning model inspired by the structure and function of the human brain that was introduced in the 1950s. In its simplest form, a neural network consists of an array of variables called "neurons" that hold individual values of an input sample. This array, known as the input layer, is connected to a sequence of intermediate arrays, referred to as *hidden layers*, that transform the input values. The last hidden layer is connected to an *output layer* that produces the result.

Each neuron in a layer is connected to every neuron in the next layer (a pattern known as a fully connected neural network), and each neuron-to-neuron connection has an associated weight parameter. In addition, each neuron in the hidden layers and the output layer has an associated bias parameter.

Figure 2.1 shows a diagram of a simple neural network with an eight-neuron input layer, three hidden layers, and a single-neuron output layer. The hidden layers do not necessarily need to be of the same dimension. A single-neuron output layer can be used to represent a binary decision (e.g., true vs false), and a multiple-neuron layer can be used to represent a wider range of outcomes. To give a concrete example, consider a neural network trained to identify if an image with 32×32 pixels represents the letter 'A' or not. In that case, a sample image can be passed to an input layer with 1024 neurons (32×32). The value of the output layer is zero or one, indicating whether the input image represents the letter 'A' or not.

A neural network is trained by iteratively updating the values of the weight and bias parameters to minimize a cost function across a vast number of training samples. This function quantifies, for each training sample, the difference between the output and the expected output. The minimization of the cost function is performed by a back-propagation

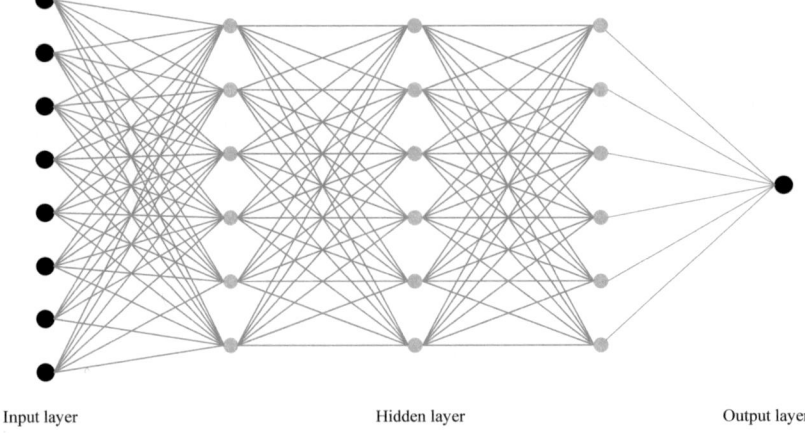

Input layer   Hidden layer   Output layer

Fig. 2.1   A simple neural network

algorithm (Rumelhart et al., 1986) that computes the negative gradient[1] of the function at each iteration and for each sample and adjusts the values of the parameters in proportion to the gradient. "Learning" in the context of neural networks means minimizing the cost function through the iterative updating of the parameters.

Early neural networks from the 1950s yielded limited results, which led to a decline in interest in the field for several decades. A resurgence of attention occurred in the 1980s with the rediscovery of the back-propagation algorithm and other algorithmic improvements that allowed neural networks to learn effectively.

In the 1990s and 2000s, the commercial introduction of graphic processing units (GPUs)—hardware initially developed for video rendering—and the development of parallel computing techniques enabled faster training of neural networks. The increased availability of computing power, algorithmic improvements, and larger datasets have facilitated the development of more complex neural network architectures, such as convolutional neural networks (CNNs) and recurrent neural networks (RNNs). The former are used primarily in computer-vision applications such as image recognition and object detection. In contrast, RNNs are used to process sequential data such as time series or human language, in which the order of the elements in the data conveys important information.

In the 2010s, further improvements in hardware and software, advances in training techniques, and more available data made it possible to develop deep neural networks with even more layers and complex architectures that increased their predictive performance and significantly expanded the use of these models in real-world applications (Dean, 2022).

TRANSFORMER ARCHITECTURE AND LLMs

A transformative event occurred in 2017 with the introduction of the Transformer architecture, a deep neural network optimized for parallelized training on large volumes of text (Vaswani et al., 2017). Two notable design contributions were the integration of positional encoding and a self-attention mechanism. Positional encoding is a technique that

---

[1] The gradient of a function indicates the direction of the steepest increase of the function. The negative gradient indicates the direction of the steepest decrease.

adds information about the order of words to the input data, which allows the neural network to learn sequence information from the data. Attention mechanisms allow models to map an input sequence to an output sequence (for tasks such as language translation) to assign more weight to relevant parts of the input sequence when generating the output sequence. Self-attention is a variation of the mechanism relating different elements of a single sequence. The parallelization of training allowed training on vast amounts of data, which gave transformer neural networks the ability to capture a statistical representation of language. An LLM is a statistical representation of language obtained from training and fine-tuning a neural network using vast amounts of language data. Although the Transformer architecture was initially intended for translation, the language representation in LLMs makes them highly effective across a wide range of language tasks, such as reading comprehension, summarization, translation, and question answering (Radford et al., 2018, 2019). These capabilities improve with larger models (Brown et al., 2020).

The development of LLM-based applications involves two phases: pretraining to generate a general language representation and fine-tuning for specific functions, such as a conversational chatbot that follows instructions. An LLM is pretrained via self-supervised learning (SSL), a technique in which the model is trained to predict parts of the input data from other parts of the same input. For example, the model is trained to predict the word "mat" in the input sentence "The cat sat on the [MASK]" with the word masked. The technique vastly increases the amount of data available for pretraining since manually labeled datasets are not needed. Fine-tuning to follow human instructions, for example, is performed via reinforcement learning with human feedback (RLHF) or similar techniques that use human preferences as a reward signal to fine-tune the model (Ouyang et al., 2022).

The first large-scale application of the Transformer architecture was Google's BERT (Devlin et al., 2019), which was deployed in 2019 to improve the relevance of search engine results. OpenAI launched ChatGPT in November 2022, and by February 2023, it surpassed 100 million monthly active users, setting the record for the fastest-growing consumer application in history at the time. In March 2023, OpenAI introduced the ChatGPT application programming interface (API), allowing developers to integrate its capabilities into their applications and services. Since then, diverse ecosystems of models, applications, and APIs have emerged, including Google's Gemini, Anthropic's Claude, and open-weights alternatives such as Meta's Llama and Mixtral.

Figure 2.2 graphically shows the evolution of AI and NLP since the 1950s, highlighting the pivotal developments.

EMBEDDINGS AND TEXT GENERATION

Embedding is a fundamental concept in machine learning used to represent complex data such as words, phrases, images, and sounds in a format that computers can understand and use. In this approach, words are first broken down into smaller units called tokens, which can be whole words, parts of words, or even single characters. Each token is then converted into a specific list of numbers, called a vector, of length d. The vector is the embedding of the token. The embeddings position the tokens in a d-dimensional "semantic space," where tokens with similar meanings are located close together. Early NLP models used techniques such as word2vec (Mikolov et al., 2013) and GloVe (Pennington et al., 2014) to create these embeddings. The length of the vectors is a configurable parameter and is typically in the hundreds or thousands. The embeddings from word2vec and similar algorithms proved effective in capturing relationships between words but failed to capture the more nuanced meaning of sentences and texts of arbitrary length.

LLMs address this limitation by introducing contextualized embeddings. In this approach, the embedding of a token within an input text sequence is refined through the layers of a transformer model, making it more specific to the sequence of text to which it belongs. For example, the embedding of the word "bank" will differ depending on whether the surrounding text discusses finance or a land by a river.

An LLM uses the contextualized embeddings of the tokens in the input sequence to predict the most likely token to follow in the sequence. This is done by transforming the embedding of the last token into a vector with a size equal to the number of tokens in the vocabulary (i.e., the set of all the tokens supported by the model). The values in this vector, called logits or scores, are normalized (i.e., the sum equals one) to create a probability distribution. The next token is randomly selected from this distribution.

The variability of the output is controlled through two parameters: *temperature* and *top-p*. The former is a value greater than zero that controls the shape of the probability distribution. A temperature lower

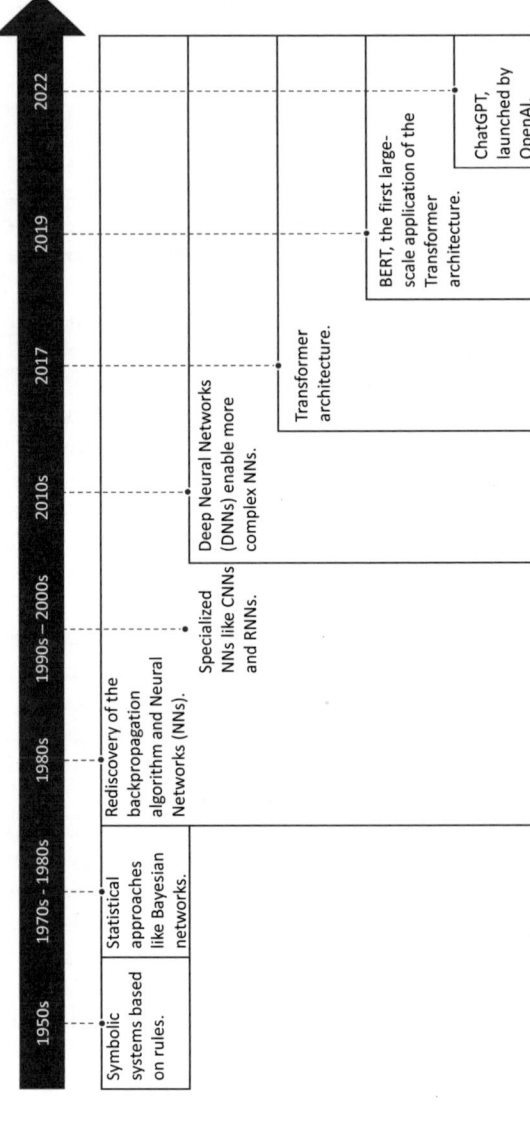

Fig. 2.2 Evolution of AI and NLP

than one amplifies the scores of the more likely tokens, causing the model to prefer them in the random selection. A temperature greater than one makes the differences between scores smaller, giving less likely tokens a greater chance of being selected, which results in more random and creative text. A temperature equal to one maintains the shape of the probability distribution. The top-p parameter is used to restrict the set of tokens to select from. Its value is greater than zero and smaller than 100%. If top-p is, for example, 90%, and the top three tokens have probabilities of 50%, 30%, and 10%, the model will randomly select the next token from this subset.

Open-Source, Open-Weights, and Proprietary LLMs

Large language models can be categorized by the approach taken to share information about them. Open-source LLMs publish their full code, architecture, training data, and weights under permissive licenses that allow researchers to inspect, modify, and extend the models freely. The premise of open-source models is that their development increases transparency, access, safety, and other critical dimensions of this technology. An example of an open-source model is the open language model (OLMO) developed by the Allen Institute for AI. The OLMo and olmes GitHub repositories contain the information needed to reproduce the training, fine-tuning, and evaluation of the different variants of the model. The model is released under an Apache 2.0 license, a permissive license whose main condition is the preservation of license and copyright notices.

Unlike open-source models, open-weights LLMs publish their trained parameter values (weights) and allow users to run and fine-tune models but keep the training datasets and code proprietary and use more restrictive licenses. A prominent example of this type of model is Meta's LLaMA family of models. The Open Source Initiative does not approve the Llama 4 license as an open-source license, and it is restrictive in different ways. For example, its acceptable use policy has a defined set of prohibited uses, and the rights granted under section 2.1(a) of the license are not granted for multimodal versions of the model to individuals in the European Union, which can be a limitation for global usability.

Proprietary models expose neither code nor weights and are typically offered only via hosted APIs or services. Prominent proprietary models publish "system cards" describing the models' architecture, training data, and capabilities with varying levels of detail. Examples include Anthropic's Claude 4, Google's Gemini 2.5 Pro Preview, and OpenAI's o3/o4-mini system cards. The documents describe evaluations of the models' performance against various benchmarks and internal testing, highlighting improvements and remaining limitations. A significant portion of each document focuses on safety evaluations, covering areas such as disallowed content, hallucinations, and potential risks such as AI self-improvement, cybersecurity, and risks related to biological and chemical use.

In this book, we provide practical guidance and examples on how to use open-source, open-weights, and proprietary LLMs, empowering you to make informed decisions and leverage these tools for a variety of applications.

LIMITATIONS OF LLMS

Large language models present several critical limitations that researchers need to address to harness their benefits without compromising the integrity of their research.

A first limitation is hallucinations, a phenomenon where LLMs generate content that appears plausible but is nonfactual or unfaithful to the provided source or instructions (Huang et al., 2025). This is a significant issue since misleading information can spread false beliefs or cause harm. Huang et al. (2025) define two primary types: factuality and faithfulness hallucinations. The former refers to discrepancies between the output of a model and verifiable real-world facts. The latter refers to a lack of self-consistency within the generated output or divergences between the output and the user input or the provided context. Hallucinations stem from issues at every stage of development: data, training, and inference. To combat this, mitigation strategies are tailored to each source. These include using high-quality data and techniques such as retrieval-augmented generation (RAG), fine-tuning models to correct for misalignments, and improving decoding methods to ensure that the output is more realistic.

A second limitation is the potential for biases. In the context of LLMs, biases refer to disparate model outcomes between social groups that arise from historical and structural power asymmetries (Gallegos et al., 2024). Biases are categorized into representational harms, such as misrepresentation, stereotyping, derogatory language, or exclusionary norms, and allocational harms, such as direct and indirect discrimination. Gallegos et al. (2024) define taxonomies of metrics and datasets for bias evaluation and a taxonomy of techniques for bias mitigation on the basis of the intervention stage: modifying model inputs, the training process, the inference behavior, or the model outputs.

Another limitation is reasoning, which is the cognitive process of deriving conclusions from premises or evidence. LLMs excel at recognizing language patterns and have shown an emergent ability to "reason" when they are large enough. However, it remains unclear whether these models can achieve acceptable performance in common reasoning tasks. Unlike formal reasoning techniques such as symbolic logic and knowledge graphs, which incorporate structured knowledge representations, LLMs rely on a statistical representation of language and nondeterministic methods for inference. Specific factors that limit the reasoning ability of LLMs include hallucinations, lack of explicit memory, biases, and limited generalizability across domains. Approaches to improve this ability include fine-tuning LLMs with structured reasoning data, enhancing the models with knowledge retrieval mechanisms, combining neural networks with symbolic reasoning, and, finally, self-supervised and reinforcement learning techniques (Patil & Jadon, 2025).

Another limitation is the lack of transparency and explainability. This refers to the inability to fully understand why an LLM produces a specific output, which poses the risk of generating harmful content and makes it difficult to build trust in critical applications. Explainability allows end users to grasp the capabilities, limitations, and flaws of a model. It also helps researchers and developers identify biases, risks, and areas for performance improvement and to develop safety mechanisms. Zhao et al. (2024) categorize LLM explainability techniques on the basis of two goals: understanding how pretraining and fine-tuning build language comprehension and analyzing how pretrained knowledge is applied in response to prompts. Research also highlights the importance of evaluating these explanations for their plausibility and faithfulness to the model's actual decision-making process (Zhao et al., 2024).

Another limitation is the high cost and energy consumption of LLMs. Training and serving very large language models require large amounts of computational resources and energy, contributing to environmental concerns and potentially limiting accessibility for smaller organizations or individuals. For example, the cost of training GPT-4 was estimated to be more than $100 million. In general, training costs include the cost of computing, storing, and networking hardware; the datacenter space and power needed by the equipment; the cost of acquiring and preparing data; and the labor costs of fine-tuning techniques such as reinforcement learning with human feedback (RLHF).

A final important limitation is prompt sensitivity, which refers to how much the output of a language model changes on the basis of superficial semantically equivalent variations of an input prompt. This behavior can make debugging and reproducibility difficult for developers and ultimately affect the reliability of real-world applications. However, distinguishing unwanted from necessary sensitivity is important. A model must be robust to semantically equivalent prompts but must produce a different output if the meaning of the prompt or the requested task changes significantly. Importantly, clear, specific, and well-structured prompts generally yield the most consistent results. Developers mitigate prompt sensitivity in large language models (LLMs) through several key techniques. They use large, diverse datasets and supervised fine-tuning to help the model understand the true meaning behind prompts rather than just word correlations. Furthermore, reinforcement learning with human feedback (RLHF) aligns the model to be more consistent and helpful. Moreover, prompt analysis mechanisms can be used as a final safety measure to check for semantic equivalence and filter inappropriate queries.

These factors compound an ethical risk of misuse and misinformation in areas of significant societal impact, such as marketing, finance, and business governance. Researchers need to treat LLM outputs with care. In practical terms, this requires establishing verification and ethical oversight in research projects. This book provides several guidelines and considerations when implementing these tools. We also encourage researchers to stay abreast of ongoing research on LLM limitations and integrate the outcome of these efforts into their work. In the following chapters, we discuss how these tools have been integrated into qualitative research recently and important ethical considerations when incorporating them into research projects.

References

Bolstad, W. M., & Curran, J. M. (2017). *Introduction to Bayesian statistics* (3rd ed.). Wiley.

Brown, T., Mann, B., Ryder, N., Subbiah, M., Kaplan, J. D., Dhariwal, P., Neelakantan, A., Shyam, P., Sastry, G., Askell, A., Agarwal, S., Herbert-Voss, A., Krueger, G., Henighan, T., Child, R., Ramesh, A., Ziegler,

D., Wu, J., Winter, C., ... Amodei, D. (2020). Language models are few-shot learners. *Advances in Neural Information Processing Systems, 33*, 1877–1901. https://proceedings.neurips.cc/paper_files/paper/2020/hash/1457c0d6bfcb4967418bfb8ac142f64a-Abstract.html

Dean, J. (2022). A golden decade of deep learning: Computing systems & applications. *Daedalus, 151*(2), 58–74. https://doi.org/10.1162/daed_a_01900

Devlin, J., Chang, M.-W., Lee, K., & Toutanova, K. (2019). Bert: Pre-training of deep bidirectional transformers for language understanding. *arXiv Preprint*: arXiv:1810.04805. https://doi.org/10.48550/arXiv.1810.04805

Gallegos, I. O., Rossi, R. A., Barrow, J., Tanjim, M. M., Kim, S., Dernoncourt, F., Yu, T., Zhang, R., & Ahmed, N. K. (2024). Bias and fairness in large language models: A survey. *Computational Linguistics, 50*(3), 1097–1179. https://doi.org/10.1162/coli_a_00524

Green, A., Tillett, W., McHugh, N., Smith, T., & The PROMPT Study Group. (2022). Using Bayesian networks to identify musculoskeletal symptoms influencing the risk of developing psoriatic arthritis in people with psoriasis. *Rheumatology, 61*(2), 581–590. https://doi.org/10.1093/rheumatology/keab310

Huang, L., Yu, W., Ma, W., Zhong, W., Feng, Z., Wang, H., Chen, Q., Peng, W., Feng, X., Qin, B., & Liu, T. (2025). A survey on hallucination in large language models: Principles, taxonomy, challenges, and open questions. *ACM Transactions on Information Systems, 43*(2), 1–55, Article 42. https://doi.org/10.1145/3703155

McClintock, B. T., & Michelot, T. (2018). MomentuHMM: R package for generalized hidden Markov models of animal movement. *Methods in Ecology and Evolution, 9*(6), 1518–1530. https://doi.org/10.1111/2041-210X.12995

Mikolov, T., Sutskever, I., Chen, K., Corrado, G. S., & Dean, J. (2013). Distributed representations of words and phrases and their compositionality. *Advances in Neural Information Processing Systems, 26*, 3111–3119.

Ouyang, L., Wu, J., Jiang, X., Almeida, D., Wainwright, C. L., Mishkin, P., Zhang, C., Agarwal, S., Slama, K., Ray, A., Schulman, J., Hilton, J., Kelton, F., Miller, L., Simens, M., Askell, A., Welinder, P., Christiano, P., Leike, J., & Lowe, R. (2022). Training language models to follow instructions with human feedback. *Advances in Neural Information Processing Systems*, 27730–27744.

Patil, A., & Jadon, A. (2025). *Advancing reasoning in large language models: Promising methods and approaches* (No. arXiv:2502.03671). https://doi.org/10.48550/arXiv.2502.03671

Peal, J. (1985). Bayesian networks: A model of self-activated memory for evidential reasoning. *Proceedings of the Annual Meeting of the Cognitive Science Society, 7*. https://escholarship.org/uc/item/0vr7830n

Pennington, J., Socher, R., & Manning, C. (2014). GloVe: Global vectors for word representation. In A. Moschitti, B. Pang, & W. Daelemans (Eds.), *Proceedings of the 2014 Conference on Empirical Methods in Natural Language Processing (EMNLP)* (pp. 1532–1543). Association for Computational Linguistics. https://doi.org/10.3115/v1/D14-1162

Rabiner, L. R. (1989). A tutorial on hidden Markov models and selected applications in speech recognition. *Proceedings of the IEEE, 77*(2), 257–286. https://doi.org/10.1109/5.18626

Radford, A., Narasimhan, K., Salimans, T., & Sutskever, I. (2018). Improving language understanding by generative pre-training. *OpenAI Pre-Print*.

Radford, A., Wu, J., Child, R., Luan, D., Amodei, D., & Sutskever, I. (2019). Language models are unsupervised multitask learners. *OpenAI Pre-Print*.

Rumelhart, D. E., Hinton, G. E., & Williams, R. J. (1986). Learning representations by back-propagating errors. *Nature, 323*(6088), 533–536. https://doi.org/10.1038/323533a0

Vaswani, A., Shazeer, N., Parmar, N., Uszkoreit, J., Jones, L., Gomez, A. N., Kaiser, Ł., & Polosukhin, I. (2017). Attention is all you need. *Advances in Neural Information Processing Systems, 30*, 6000–6010. https://proceedings.neurips.cc/paper/2017/file/3f5ee243547dee91fbd053c1c4a845aa-Paper.pdf

Zhao, H., Chen, H., Yang, F., Liu, N., Deng, H., Cai, H., Wang, S., Yin, D., & Du, M. (2024). Explainability for large language models: A survey. *ACM Transactions on Intelligent Systems and Technology, 15*(2), 20:1–38, Article 20. https://doi.org/10.1145/3639372

CHAPTER 3

Natural Language Processing in Management Research

Abstract This chapter highlights the evolving role of natural language processing (NLP) in management research. Although NLP has been utilized for decades, its full potential remains largely untapped, primarily concentrated in information systems and marketing for quantitative analysis. The chapter discusses how advancements in large language models (LLMs) have facilitated the integration of sophisticated NLP algorithms into qualitative research, enabling a more nuanced analysis of contextual meaning and the potential for richer theory development. Recent studies employing mixed-method approaches have demonstrated the ability of LLMs to enhance qualitative analysis, providing researchers with examples of the application of LLMs in qualitative research.

Keywords Qualitative analysis · Natural language processing · Large language models

The importance of AI for data analysis in management research has increased over the years. In particular, NLP has been utilized in management research for several decades, enabling the automated analysis of various textual data sources, such as annual reports, press releases, and social media posts (Kobayashi et al., 2018). By automating text analysis tasks, NLP has facilitated research, enabling researchers to analyze large corpora efficiently and reducing the burden of manual data processing

© The Author(s) 2026
D. Garcia Quevedo and J. Kuri, *AI for Qualitative Research*,
https://doi.org/10.1007/978-3-032-08872-7_3

23

(Kang et al., 2020). Consequently, NLP has been recognized as a valuable tool for advancing theory-building within management research.

However, the full potential of NLP remains largely untapped in this field. While the application of NLP in management research has grown, its utilization remains concentrated primarily within the areas of information systems and marketing research, which are used primarily for quantitative analysis (Kang et al., 2020). Furthermore, the field has historically focused on specific tasks, such as sentiment analysis to determine the emotional tone of a text and topic modeling to identify underlying themes, neglecting the diverse and rapidly evolving set of available NLP tasks.

As discussed in the previous chapter, NLP has benefited from more accessible and sophisticated algorithms leveraging LLMs. These advancements offer new opportunities to enhance management research. By thoughtfully integrating LLM-based algorithms for NLP into their methodological toolkit, management researchers can open novel pathways for theory development.

In the following section, we explore how NLP tasks have been utilized for qualitative research recently. Notably, with the advent of LLMs, qualitative researchers have explored the capabilities of these tools for qualitative analysis.

NLP in Qualitative Research Today

Qualitative researchers have historically been hesitant to adopt computational methods since they are often perceived as incompatible with interpretative analysis. Early NLP models have further reinforced this reluctance because of their limited capacity to understand context and nuance. As discussed in the previous chapter, previous NLP models were based on statistics, syntax, and grammar rules, primarily using dictionaries to identify similar themes or create classifications. As such, qualitative researchers have used them as preprocessing tools to find general themes or predefined categories. Thus, they are mainly used to perform thematic analysis on large datasets (Kobayashi et al., 2018). Qualitative researchers who favor close contact with data, considering nuance, subtilities, and context, found early NLP models to be very limited.

With advancements in recent years, LLMs can now capture semantic meaning, subtle nuance, and context on vast unstructured text corpora. LLMs have overcome the limitations of previous NLP models, paving the way for new opportunities in qualitative research. Owing to these advancements, the acceptance of these new technologies has shifted recently (Feuston & Brubaker, 2021). Qualitative researchers have ventured into exploring how to leverage these capabilities following an inductive approach, which requires close contact with the data to capture contextual meaning and nuance. LLMs allow qualitative researchers to move beyond traditional automatic thematic text analysis.

Recognizing the potential of NLP, some qualitative scholars have championed its use as a rigorous methodological tool (e.g., Abram et al., 2020; Kang et al., 2020; Nelson, 2020). Moreover, several studies have validated the effectiveness and speed of mixed-method approaches. For example, Krlev et al. (2025) used a combination of methods to analyze 1,441 literature review articles in management research. They employed a mixed-method approach, combining topic modeling to identify broad themes and interpretive qualitative analysis to understand specific meanings, arguments, and nuances. This approach allowed for a comprehensive understanding of the different types of literature reviews used in management research (Krlev et al., 2025). Another example is Aranda et al. (2021). They proposed a mixed-method approach integrating topic modeling in critical discourse analysis. They recognize the significant challenge that qualitative researchers encounter when manually processing and analyzing extensive, unstructured datasets (Aranda et al., 2021). In their model, Aranda et al. (2021) use topic modeling to inform the qualitative interpretation of data in a sequential process that guides and informs each iteration. These authors favor the use of modern techniques to complement qualitative analysis, citing them as being time and resource efficient.

The accessibility of chatbots powered by LLMs such as OpenAI's ChatGPT and Google's Gemini has accelerated this new approach to inductive analysis. Owing to the novelty of LLMs, there is limited published research in Management about their use in qualitative research. However, recent studies have explored the potential and limitations of employing LLM chatbots following a qualitative approach. For example, Hayes (2025) proposed that qualitative researchers can interact with their data through prompts via chatbots, where the researcher can ask targeted questions for contextual insights and refine theoretical connections. The author argues that this conversational process can accelerate coding and theme identification, as well as provide new interpretative angles and contrasting viewpoints (Hayes, 2025).

Another example is Hamilton et al. (2023). Their study uses a phenomenological approach to data analysis, comparing the emergent themes generated by human coders and ChatGPT. They found that Chat-GPT's generated themes tend to be specific to the participant's circumstances and immediate concerns, thus disregarding nuanced context and subtleties. On the other hand, the human research team was able to identify comprehensive themes by taking into account more contextual knowledge about the participants (Hamilton et al., 2023). Another interesting example is a study conducted by Morgan (2023), which compared previous analyses with ChatGPT's output. The author argues that ChatGPT provides valuable insights during the analytical process. However, it tends to emphasize generic aspects of the data, lacking contextualization and the ability to recognize subtle and interpretative themes (Morgan, 2023). These studies conclude that AI has the potential to reduce time-consuming tasks, but it should be seen as a complementary tool rather than a means of interpretation.

Other research fields have increasingly explored the possibilities and limitations of these tools in qualitative research. In the field of sociology, Nelson (2020, p. 5) proposed a methodology for "computational grounded theory research." The author advocates for computer-assisted content analysis to incorporate an extra layer of rigor, reliability, reproducibility, and scalability in inductive analysis (Nelson, 2020). In particular, the field of Computer Science has been actively investigating the applications and limitations of LLMs for qualitative approaches. For example, Zhang et al. (2024) developed a ChatGPT-based framework to explore the experiences of thirteen qualitative researchers using LLM prompting for data analysis. They emphasize the importance of enhancing transparency, offering guidance on prompt design, and strengthening researchers' understanding of the potential and limitations of LLMs, which will lead to improved results (Zhang et al., 2024).

These scholars advocate the use of LLMs as a complement to the analytical expertise of qualitative researchers, highlighting their potential to enhance analytical rigor and facilitate the theoretical process. However, they acknowledge that LLMs are deprived of interpretative capabilities. Only researchers can provide a deeper, interpretive, and genuine understanding of social phenomena. As the use of LLMs for qualitative analysis has gained traction, the next section explores several potential applications in this area.

LLM Applications in Qualitative Research

This section explores how LLM-based algorithms for NLP tasks can be used to enhance inductive qualitative analysis. LLMs enhance the performance of traditional NLP tasks, enabling new applications and facilitating the integration of multiple tasks into systems with sophisticated capabilities. Researchers can utilize these systems to analyze vast amounts of unstructured data, thereby increasing the breadth and depth of their inductive qualitative research projects.

Given the vast amount of online data available and its inherently unstructured nature, computational power becomes indispensable for accessing it (Garcia Quevedo et al., 2025). As such, LLM-based NLP algorithms offer a significant advantage. By leveraging the augmentation and automation capabilities of these algorithms, researchers can effectively incorporate extensive datasets into their projects, thereby expanding the scope of qualitative inquiry.

Qualitative researchers can leverage LLMs by combining their multiple capabilities. They can be used as exploratory tools via text exploration and summarization. Their generative capabilities can be leveraged for in-depth exploration and interrogation of the dataset through retrieved-augmented generation (RAG). Furthermore, LLMs excel at categorizing data, capturing language nuances and context, and identifying implicit patterns in large datasets. Below, we delve deeper into those capabilities and provide examples of their application.

Text Exploration and Summarization

In the initial stage of data analysis, researchers need to gain a general understanding of the dataset. Foundational techniques such as word frequency and word similarity analyses serve as valuable steps for obtaining a preliminary understanding of the data composition. Word frequency analysis, by revealing the most prevalent words within a text, offers a snapshot of the dominant ideas. Word similarity analysis, which examines the semantic relationships between words, finds contextual nuances and underlying connections within the data. These basic steps can play a crucial role in validating the dataset's relevance to a specific research question.

LLMs can significantly facilitate the exploratory phase of data analysis. Owing to their ability to generate coherent and contextually relevant text,

LLMs enable the application of text summarization as an efficient tool for rapidly processing and comprehending extensive datasets. Text summarization goes beyond the extraction of key sentences. It involves the generation of a concise yet comprehensive overview that can capture the essence of the data. This allows researchers to quickly grasp the general ideas embedded in the data and identify potential areas of interest, facilitating a more focused and targeted analysis. Like with word-frequency and similarity analyses, text summarization can also serve as a preliminary validation step, allowing researchers to assess the dataset's content and relevance quickly before committing to more in-depth, resource-intensive inductive analysis.

LLMs can effectively navigate and explore large datasets, providing essential general insights into their content and composition. This preliminary exploration allows researchers to make informed decisions about the suitability of the data for their research goals and to allocate resources efficiently.

Morgan (2023) provides a good example of how to utilize LLMs to explore and further investigate a dataset via simple prompts, leveraging the summarization capabilities of LLMs. In this study, the author utilized ChatGPT to query a qualitative dataset and then built upon those outputs to further explore the dataset. ChatGPT was able to summarize the topic of the entire dataset, provide a list of the main topics, and summarize the content of each topic. The author argues that ChatGPT provides valuable insights during the analytical process (Morgan, 2023).

Data Retrieval and Augmentation

Retrieval-augmented generation (RAG) introduces a transformative approach to analyzing large corpora within qualitative research, shifting from traditional linear analysis to a dynamic, interactive question-and-answer tool. RAG allows researchers to pinpoint specific pieces of information and ask questions about their interconnectedness within the broader context of the data. By enabling targeted information retrieval, RAG facilitates the identification of nuanced relationships and patterns that might remain obscured in conventional analytical processes.

RAG can also be integrated into an in-depth exploratory phase, complementing exploratory analysis and summarization. Moreover, the iterative nature of RAG lends itself particularly well to enhancing and refining the analytical process. Researchers can employ RAG to progressively interrogate the data, uncovering layers of meaning and iteratively adjusting their interpretations. This iterative approach not only streamlines the discovery of relevant information but also promotes a deeper, more comprehensive understanding of the dataset.

Furthermore, RAG can serve as a powerful tool for challenging and validating existing conclusions. By posing specific questions to the data, researchers can actively seek evidence that either supports or contradicts their initial interpretations. This approach can foster intellectual rigor and help mitigate potential biases, ensuring that conclusions are grounded in robust data analysis. The ability to interrogate the corpus in this manner significantly strengthens the credibility and reliability of qualitative research findings.

By leveraging RAG to navigate the data, researchers can develop a more informed and nuanced analytical framework, laying the groundwork for a more insightful and robust inductive analysis. In summary, RAG allows qualitative researchers to engage with large datasets in a more dynamic, interactive, and rigorous manner, facilitating the discovery of deeper insights and paving the way for more robust and comprehensive analysis.

An example of RAG's capabilities is presented in the study of Bhaduri et al. (2024). The authors used an open-source dataset of interview transcripts from educators discussing their use of open educational practices. The researchers employed RAG to conduct a thematic analysis of the interview transcripts. This process combines the capabilities of an LLM with those of a retrieval system to source and integrate additional information into its responses. By doing so, the researchers were able to identify topics of interest from the interview transcripts with significant coverage compared with the manually generated topics (Bhaduri et al., 2024).

Classification and Clustering Analysis

Inductive analyses are fundamentally driven by classification, the discovery of meaningful patterns, and the subsequent interpretation of data to provide an explanation for social phenomena (Saldaña, 2013). This process, which is inherently iterative, requires researchers to meticulously examine data, identify recurring themes, and develop conceptual frameworks that illuminate the underlying meanings. LLMs present a significant advancement, offering customizable capabilities that can substantially streamline and enhance inductive analysis.

The inherent ability of LLMs to excel at classification and clustering tasks is particularly noteworthy. By leveraging their sophisticated pattern recognition and semantic understanding, LLMs can efficiently categorize and group data on the basis of research-defined criteria. This automation significantly reduces the time and effort traditionally allocated to manual classification, enabling researchers to focus on higher-level interpretive tasks. For example, LLMs can be fine-tuned to classify textual data based on specific themes, sentiments, or discourse patterns, providing a structured foundation for subsequent inductive analysis.

Furthermore, the adaptability of LLMs allows seamless customization to meet the specific needs of diverse research projects. Researchers can train LLMs on domain-specific datasets, tailoring their classification capabilities to the unique characteristics of their data. This customization ensures that the algorithms accurately reflect the nuances of the research question, leading to more precise and relevant classifications. The ability to define and refine classification schemes dynamically empowers researchers to explore data from multiple perspectives, facilitating the discovery of complex and interwoven patterns.

Beyond mere classification, LLMs can also contribute to the identification of emergent patterns and relationships within the data. By analyzing the co-occurrence of themes and concepts, LLMs can reveal underlying patterns and connections that might not be immediately apparent to researchers. This capability is particularly valuable in inductive analysis, where the goal is to uncover novel insights and develop grounded theories.

Owing to their customizable classification and pattern recognition capabilities, LLMs serve as powerful tools for inductive qualitative research. LLMs alleviate these tasks, ultimately freeing researchers from engaging in more in-depth and nuanced interpretive analyses, leading to richer and more insightful research outcomes.

In their study, Gamieldien et al. (2023) compared clustering techniques using LLMs with manual coding analysis. They utilized a pretrained LLM in clustering to find the underlying topics. Then, they passed these clusters to GPT 3.5 for summarization. Using this method, they analyzed reflections written by 3,800 students after their grade exams. They compared the results with the manual coding of a subset of

270 reflections. They reported a high level of agreement between LLM-assisted clustering and manual coding. They noted an increased level of granularity offered by the LLM-assisted method, providing a more nuanced understanding of student responses. This finding highlights the potential of LLMs to uncover detailed patterns within data, providing richer insights (Gamieldien et al., 2023).

Even though LLMs are powerful tools that can be leveraged at various levels and for diverse purposes throughout the research process, researchers should consider the ethical implications of this technology. Applying different LLM-based algorithms for NLP requires exploring the ethical challenges of using these tools. As such, the following chapter provides ideas and reflections to consider when deploying AI for research projects.

References

Abram, M. D., Mancini, K. T., & Parker, R. D. (2020). Methods to integrate natural language processing into qualitative research. *International Journal of Qualitative Methods, 19*, 1609406920984608. https://doi.org/10.1177/1609406920984608

Aranda, A. M., Sele, K., Etchanchu, H., Guyt, J. Y., & Vaara, E. (2021). From big data to rich theory: Integrating critical discourse analysis with structural topic modeling. *European Management Review, 18*(3), 197–214. https://doi.org/10.1111/emre.12452

Bhaduri, S., Kapoor, S., Gil, A., Mittal, A., & Mulkar, R. (2024). *Reconciling methodological paradigms: Employing large language models as novice qualitative research assistants in talent management research* (No. arXiv:2408.11043). arXiv. https://doi.org/10.48550/arXiv.2408.11043

Feuston, J. L., & Brubaker, J. R. (2021). Putting tools in their place: The role of time and perspective in human-AI collaboration for qualitative analysis. *Proceedings of the ACM on Human-Computer Interaction, 5*(CSCW2), 1–25. https://doi.org/10.1145/3479856

Gamieldien, Y., Case, J. M., & Katz, A. (2023). *Advancing qualitative analysis: An exploration of the potential of generative AI and NLP in thematic coding* (SSRN Scholarly Paper No. 4487768). Social Science Research Network. https://doi.org/10.2139/ssrn.4487768

Garcia Quevedo, D., Glaser, A., & Verzat, C. (2025). Enhancing theorization using artificial intelligence: Leveraging large language models for qualitative analysis of online data. *Organizational Research Methods, 29*(1), 92-112. https://doi.org/10.1177/10944281251339144

Hamilton, L., Elliott, D., Quick, A., Smith, S., & Choplin, V. (2023). Exploring the use of AI in qualitative analysis: A comparative study of guaranteed income data. *International Journal of Qualitative Methods*, *22*, 16094069231201504. https://doi.org/10.1177/16094069231201504

Hayes, A. S. (2025). "Conversing" with qualitative data: Enhancing qualitative research through large language models (LLMs). *International Journal of Qualitative Methods*, *24*, 16094069251322346. https://doi.org/10.1177/16094069251322346

Kang, Y., Cai, Z., Tan, C.-W., Huang, Q., & Liu, H. (2020). Natural language processing (NLP) in management research: A literature review. *Journal of Management Analytics*, *7*(2), 139–172. https://doi.org/10.1080/23270012.2020.1756939

Kobayashi, V. B., Mol, S. T., Berkers, H. A., Kismihók, G., & Den Hartog, D. N. (2018). Text mining in organizational research. *Organizational Research Methods*, *21*(3), 733–765. https://doi.org/10.1177/1094428117722619

Krlev, G., Hannigan, T., & Spicer, A. (2025). What makes a good review article? Empirical evidence from management and organization research. *Academy of Management Annals*, *19*(1), 1–28. https://doi.org/10.5465/annals.2021.0051

Morgan, D. L. (2023). Exploring the use of artificial intelligence for qualitative data analysis: The case of ChatGPT. *International Journal of Qualitative Methods*, *22*, 16094069231211248. https://doi.org/10.1177/16094069231211248

Nelson, L. K. (2020). Computational grounded theory: A methodological framework. *Sociological Methods & Research*, *49*(1), 3–42. https://doi.org/10.1177/0049124117729703

Saldaña, J. (2013). *The coding manual for qualitative researchers* (2nd ed.). Sage.

Zhang, H., Wu, C., Xie, J., Lyu, Y., Cai, J., & Carroll, J. M. (2024). *Redefining qualitative analysis in the ai era: Utilizing ChatGPT for efficient thematic analysis* (No. arXiv:2309.10771). arXiv. http://arxiv.org/abs/2309.10771

CHAPTER 4

Ethical Considerations

Abstract This chapter addresses the ethical implications of employing large language models (LLMs) in research contexts, highlighting the increasing importance of responsible artificial intelligence (AI) use. By focusing on the integration of LLMs in the context of research methodologies, this chapter outlines specific ethical challenges, including algorithmic bias, data privacy concerns, and the inherent lack of transparency and explainability in LLM outputs. This emphasizes the necessity for researchers to rigorously validate LLM-generated outputs and maintain a balance between leveraging the efficiency of AI and preserving the richness of qualitative analysis. Ultimately, the chapter advocates for a knowledgeable and critical approach to using LLMs, fostering an informed research community that values ethical standards in the application of AI technologies.

Keywords Ethical challenges · Artificial intelligence · Large language models

The discourse surrounding ethics in AI has experienced a significant surge in both the public and academic spheres in recent years (D'Cruz et al., 2022). This conversation has been further amplified by the widespread accessibility of LLMs through user-friendly web applications and application programming interfaces (APIs). As these tools become increasingly

© The Author(s) 2026   35
D. Garcia Quevedo and J. Kuri, *AI for Qualitative Research*,
https://doi.org/10.1007/978-3-032-08872-7_4

integrated into various aspects of society, the ethical implications of their deployment have moved to the forefront of discussions among policymakers, business leaders, and academics. These stakeholders are actively engaged in developing robust guidelines and guardrails to ensure the fair, safe, ethical, and responsible development and deployment of AI technologies.

AI has been commonly used as an umbrella term encompassing a diverse array of technologies and applications, each posing unique safety and ethical challenges. As Slattery et al. (2024) highlight, these considerations manifest at multiple levels, spanning the entire lifecycle of AI systems. For example, in the conception and development phase, critical attention must be given to data privacy. This includes ensuring informed consent, safeguarding sensitive information, and mitigating potential biases inherent in training data. However, the ethical landscape extends beyond data privacy and encompasses the deployment phase, where the potential for misuse becomes a paramount concern. Here, ethical concerns shift to preventing the application of LLMs and other AI technologies for malicious purposes, such as the generation of disinformation or the creation of deepfakes (Slattery et al., 2024).

As the ethical considerations surrounding AI are multifaceted, from the initial stages of model development to the long-term implications of widespread deployment, this chapter does not aim to provide an exhaustive exploration of ethical grounds. Instead, this chapter's focus is deliberately narrowed to address the specific risks that arise when LLMs are employed as tools within research contexts. This focus stems from the fundamental assumption that AI is utilized in this context with the explicit objective of expanding our understanding of complex social phenomena, thereby contributing to the advancement of knowledge and society. By limiting our discussion to the intersection of LLMs and research methodologies, we can explore the unique challenges and considerations that researchers must address.

This delineation is not meant to diminish the importance of the broader ethical debates surrounding AI. Instead, it acknowledges the distinct set of challenges that emerge when LLMs are integrated into the research process. These include the potential for algorithmic bias to skew research findings, the challenges of ensuring transparency and data protection in LLM-assisted analyses, and the implications of relying on AI-generated insights in scholarly work. The first two challenges are inherent to the nature of LLMs, whereas the latter refers to the research position when these models are used. As such, this chapter addresses two types of ethical considerations: the challenges related to the models' nature—specifically, their conception, development, and deployment—and the challenges associated with the researcher's position in using these tools during the analytical process.

In the following sections, we explore these ethical considerations and conclude with a reflection on scholarly responsibility and ethical engagement with LLMs.

ETHICAL CONSIDERATIONS RELATED TO LLMs

As previously stated, extensive discussions about the risks and ethical problems related to the development and use of AI have been undertaken by researchers, governments, corporations, and the general public (D'Cruz et al., 2022). In this section, we examine factors that directly impact the validity and reliability of these models for research purposes. Therefore, we take a closer look at the potential bias and discrimination inherent in LLMs, the privacy and security concerns associated with handling data, and the lack of explicability and transparency resulting from their probabilistic and stochastic nature.

Bias and Discrimination

The pervasive issue of bias and discrimination within LLMs has become a central concern in AI research. As underscored by numerous studies, the composition of training data significantly influences LLM performance, often resulting in outputs that perpetuate and even amplify existing societal biases (Jiao et al., 2024). LLMs may accentuate stereotypes, prejudice, and the marginalization of specific demographic groups, leading to skewed interpretations and findings. Furthermore, the variability in LLM language performance across different languages, dialects, and linguistic styles introduces another layer of complexity. This disparity can lead to unequal representation and the dissemination of inaccurate or culturally insensitive information, particularly affecting underrepresented social groups.

While significant strides have been made to mitigate embedded biases within LLMs, including the implementation of debiasing techniques and the curation of more diverse training datasets, the challenge remains ongoing. Researchers must remain acutely aware of the potential for bias to permeate LLM-generated outputs. The generative capabilities of these models, while powerful, are not immune to the influence of their training data. Therefore, it is critical that knowledgeable users rigorously validate LLM responses. This validation process necessitates a thorough examination of outputs, considering the potential for biased or discriminatory content. Researchers must remain vigilant of potential biases to ensure accuracy and robustness during the analytical process.

Data privacy and Security

The imperatives of data privacy and security stand as important considerations when pretraining and fine-tuning LLMs. A central challenge lies in controlling the dissemination of personal data and mitigating the risk of generating harmful or toxic content. LLMs have demonstrated the capacity to retain and subsequently leak sensitive personal information, such as email addresses and phone numbers, within their generated outputs. This poses the risk of privacy breaches, potentially exposing individuals to identity theft, harassment, or other serious consequences. Furthermore, studies have revealed that LLMs can produce toxic output, meaning a vulgar or profane response, as often as 32% (Biswas & Talukdar, 2023).

Beyond the need for compliance with regulations (e.g., the GDPR and CCPA), ensuring the use of anonymized and nontoxic data is crucial. This mitigates bias and misrepresentation within LLMs, thereby enhancing the accuracy and reliability of the generated results. As such, the selection of training data must be conducted with meticulous care, prioritizing privacy protection and excluding potentially harmful content.

Researchers must exercise caution regarding data usage and retention practices when interacting with LLMs during data analysis. The prompts and data provided to LLMs, even temporarily, can potentially be stored or used for further model training, raising concerns about data confidentiality and security. At a minimum, researchers must guarantee that any data passed through an LLM are thoroughly anonymized and deidentified, preventing the reconstruction of personal information. This commitment to data privacy and security extends to the management of LLM outputs. Researchers must implement robust mechanisms for reviewing and filtering generated content to prevent the inadvertent release of sensitive or toxic information.

Explainability, Transparency, and Accountability

The stochastic nature of LLMs presents a significant challenge to achieving explainability, leading to transparency and accountability issues. Unlike deterministic systems, where outputs are predictable and reproducible, LLMs are models that generate responses on the basis of a statistical representation of language. This stochasticity makes it difficult to predictably relate the inputs to the output of a model and explain the content generated by an LLM. Consequently, the lack of a clear, deterministic pathway complicates efforts to explain and justify LLM-generated content, hindering transparency and accountability.

The general lack of details on the datasets and procedures used to train the models and generate outputs further exacerbates this problem. Full transparency requires that the training datasets, training methods, fine-tuning, and inference procedures be auditable and replicable by anyone interested in understanding and using the models. However, proprietary LLMs, including OpenAI's GPT suite, do not disclose this information since it is considered a source of competitive advantage. The lack of visibility hinders researchers' ability to fully comprehend the model outputs, thereby impeding their capacity to assess the reliability and potential biases of the results.

Transparency is critical for accountability. When researchers can trace the origins of model outputs and comprehend the factors influencing them, it becomes easier to identify and address potential biases or errors. By understanding the model's limitations and potential biases, researchers can make informed decisions about the reliability and validity of the outputs (Jiao et al., 2024). Therefore, in the context of research, the lack of explainability and transparency poses unique challenges. Researchers must be acutely aware of the specifications and training parameters of the LLMs that they use. Without a clear understanding of these factors, researchers risk inadvertently reproducing inherited biases or generating misleading results because of the model's original parameters. This can compromise the integrity and validity of research findings, undermining the credibility of scholarly work.

The challenges of using LLMs in research are tied to their probabilistic nature, the limited information available about how they are developed, and the ways in which researchers utilize the models in their work. Researchers should reflect on these limitations when incorporating

LLMs into research projects. The following section provides guidance to help researchers manage these challenges more effectively.

ETHICAL CONSIDERATIONS WHEN USING LLMS IN QUALITATIVE RESEARCH

The integration of AI into the scientific research process is rapidly expanding, permeating every stage from initial project conceptualization to the final dissemination of findings in publications. The allure of AI lies in its promise to significantly increase research productivity, encouraging researchers to integrate these powerful tools across all aspects of their work. However, alongside this enthusiasm, some researchers are cautioning against the potential pitfalls of overreliance on AI in the pursuit of knowledge.

Messeri and Crockett (2024) warned about the illusions of understanding and the creation of monocultures that can arise from an uncritical embrace of AI. They contend that AI tools, often presented as scientific assistants, can foster an overdependence on their outputs, leading researchers into a false sense of comprehension. The authors argue that these illusions can manifest in several ways. For example, researchers may believe that they possess a more profound understanding of a phenomenon than what is warranted by AI-driven insights. In addition, the use of AI tools poses the risk of creating scientific monocultures, in which the research community, seduced by the efficiency and apparent objectivity of AI, increasingly prioritizes research questions, methodologies, and even perspectives that are easily processed and optimized by AI. This homogenization diminishes the cognitive and cultural diversity crucial for scientific innovation, increasing the vulnerability of research to errors and biases induced by the use of AI (Messeri & Crockett, 2024). Echoing these concerns, Roberts et al. (2024) explore the risk of diminishing the skills of qualitative researchers posed by overreliance on AI and the generative capabilities of LLM assistance. They argue that while LLMs offer efficiency gains across the research pipeline, from generating interview questions to drafting publications, this assistance can subtly undermine the core skills of qualitative researchers. The authors emphasize the risk of overlooking the lack of genuine understanding, ethical sensibility, and capacity for acknowledging uncertainty due to the human-like capabilities of these models (Roberts et al., 2024).

Lindebaum and Ashraf (2024) critique the overoptimism of using AI in research, particularly in the context of organizational theory. They argue that this optimism leads to ontological neglect, where fundamental ontological questions about the nature of social reality are overlooked in the rush to adopt AI-driven methodologies. By advocating for AI as a tool to advance theory, the authors contend that researchers risk reducing the role of science to a purely positivist endeavor, prioritizing prediction over deeper understanding and explanation. They highlight that the underlying positivist paradigm embedded in AI algorithms can limit the scope for researchers to construct knowledge through diverse approaches, particularly qualitative research. In this positivist framework, the emphasis on prediction may overshadow the crucial role of social science in explaining and interpreting complex social phenomena within their specific historical and social contexts. As such, they caution against methodological monism, in which quantitative and AI-driven approaches become the dominant paradigm, potentially at the expense of qualitative research, which excels at capturing nuanced, contextualized, and subjective understandings of social realities. Furthermore, they argue that the application of positivist quality standards, such as replicability and transparency, to qualitative data can be detrimental and even dangerous. While these standards are seemingly rigorous, they may inappropriately impose standards that are not congruent with the goals and strengths of inductive research (Lindebaum & Ashraf, 2024).

This concern regarding methodological bias is echoed by Ashwin et al. (2023). Their empirical study, which focused on annotating interview transcripts with LLMs, revealed a significant risk of introducing systematic biases. They demonstrated that LLMs, while capable of processing large volumes of text data efficiently, tend to generate annotations that are less accurate than those of human experts and are systematically biased. This technical bias, stemming from the LLMs' training data and probabilistic nature, can lead to misleading interpretations and potentially skew research findings, particularly in contexts where nuanced, contextual understanding is essential. The authors highlight that LLMs, like any machine learning model, reflect the biases present in their training data, which may not adequately represent the diverse contexts and communities often central to qualitative research (Ashwin et al., 2023).

While acknowledging the potential benefits of AI in enhancing efficiency and productivity, these scholars emphasize the importance of safeguarding the plurality of approaches and methods that are essential for robust and innovative research. The challenge lies in finding a delicate equilibrium: harnessing the power of AI to advance research while consciously mitigating the epistemic risks derived from its use. Researchers must strive to find a judicious balance, strategically leveraging AI capabilities where appropriate while simultaneously safeguarding the irreplaceable value of human expertise, diverse perspectives, and critical, context-aware understanding in the pursuit of knowledge.

TOWARD AN INFORMED AND RESPONSIBLE USE OF AI

LLMs are sophisticated tools, but they do not possess the capacity for genuine interpretation. The nuanced understanding, contextualization, and interpretation remain firmly rooted in the researcher's intellectual domain. As such, this book views LLMs as powerful *tools* in the qualitative researcher's methodological toolbox and not as replacements for their critical thinking and expertise. The creativity, intellectual rigor, and interpretive depth of qualitative research can be achieved only through skilled researchers. LLMs, however, offer transformative potential to significantly *enhance* the analytical scope of qualitative research. By thoughtfully leveraging their augmentation and automation capabilities, researchers can overcome traditional limitations associated with managing and analyzing large, complex datasets. This newfound capacity allows for the incorporation of diverse data sources—encompassing textual, visual, and auditory information—into qualitative studies, paving the way for a more comprehensive and rich understanding of complex phenomena.

Our approach, therefore, advocates for a knowledge-based and critically informed integration of LLMs into the research process. This necessitates a deep understanding within the research community of the inner workings of these tools—their function and underlying algorithms. This effort can demystify the opaque "black box" of LLMs, diminishing the risk of overreliance and fostering a culture of critical engagement with their outputs. However, we do not envision a future where qualitative researchers are expected to become proficient programmers of language models. Instead, we propose a more pragmatic and empowering path: researchers should strive to understand the fundamental principles underpinning these technologies. This understanding clarifies their generative capabilities, fostering informed use and mitigating the risk of uncritically accepting AI-generated outputs. By understanding the "nuts and bolts" of LLMs, researchers can responsibly decide which models are best suited for specific projects, making informed choices about their application and interpretation.

We contend that a foundational understanding of LLM technology empowers researchers to effectively question and challenge algorithm outputs, ensuring that AI-generated insights are rigorously scrutinized and thoughtfully integrated into the broader analytical process. LLMs, while undeniably powerful, must be viewed as one component within the wide array of methodological tools available for conducting comprehensive and rigorous research.

As such, responsibility in this context begins with informed model selection. Researchers must be equipped to critically evaluate the advantages and disadvantages of various LLM models, considering factors such as training data, algorithmic biases, and intended functionalities. A deep understanding of these model-specific nuances is essential for mitigating potential pitfalls and maximizing the benefits of AI assistance while maintaining the integrity of the research process. This book, therefore, advocates for a foundational understanding of LLM technology, empowering researchers to become *educated users* able to leverage AI capabilities effectively and ethically.

By focusing on these research-specific ethical concerns, we seek to provide researchers with a comprehensive approach to responsible and ethical engagement with LLMs. Therefore, in the second part of this book, we provide a step-by-step guide for deploying LLMs for research purposes. First, we present the basics of computer programming to manipulate data via the Python language. Second, we follow Garcia Quevedo et al.'s (2025) method to use LLM-based algorithms for qualitative analysis. We aim to provide researchers with a wide range of available LLM-based algorithms and an understanding of how they work for them to decide on the set of tools that best suit their specific research needs.

REFERENCES

Ashwin, J., Chhabra, A., & Rao, V. (2023). Using large language models for qualitative analysis can introduce serious bias. arXiv:2309.17147. http://arxiv.org/abs/2309.17147

Biswas, A., & Talukdar, W. (2023). Guardrails for trust, safety, and ethical development and deployment of Large Language Models (LLM). *Journal of*

Science & Technology, *4*(6), Article 6. https://doi.org/10.55662/JST.2023. 4605

D'Cruz, P., Du, S., Noronha, E., Parboteeah, K. P., Trittin-Ulbrich, H., & Whelan, G. (2022). Technology, megatrends and work: Thoughts on the future of business ethics. *Journal of Business Ethics, 180*(3), 879–902. https://doi.org/10.1007/s10551-022-05240-9

Garcia Quevedo, D., Glaser, A., & Verzat, C. (2025). Enhancing Theorization Using Artificial Intelligence: Leveraging Large Language Models for Qualitative Analysis of Online Data. Organizational Research Methods, 29(1), 92-112.https://doi.org/10.1177/10944281251339144

Jiao, J., Afroogh, S., Xu, Y., & Phillips, C. (2024). *Navigating LLM ethics: Advancements, challenges, and future directions* (No. arXiv:2406.18841). arXiv. https://doi.org/10.48550/arXiv.2406.18841

Lindebaum, D., & Ashraf, M. (2024). The ghost in the machine, or the ghost in organizational theory? A complementary view on the use of machine learning. *Academy of Management Review, 49*(2), 445–448. https://doi.org/10.5465/amr.2021.0036

Messeri, L., & Crockett, M. J. (2024). Artificial intelligence and illusions of understanding in scientific research. *Nature, 627*(8002), 49–58. https://doi.org/10.1038/s41586-024-07146-0

Roberts, J., Baker, M., & Andrew, J. (2024). Artificial intelligence and qualitative research: The promise and perils of large language model (LLM) 'assistance.' *Critical Perspectives on Accounting, 99*, Article 102722. https://doi.org/10.1016/j.cpa.2024.102722

Slattery, P., Saeri, A. K., Grundy, E. A. C., Graham, J., Noetel, M., Uuk, R., Dao, J., Pour, S., Casper, S., & Thompson, N. (2024). *The AI risk repository: A comprehensive meta-review, database, and taxonomy of risks from artificial intelligence* (No. arXiv:2408.12622). arXiv. https://doi.org/10.48550/arXiv.2408.12622

Part II

CHAPTER 5

Systems and Tools to Use NLP and LLMs: Getting Started

Abstract This chapter introduces essential systems and tools for leveraging various natural language processing (NLP) tasks and large language models (LLMs) in qualitative analysis, emphasizing accessibility for noncoders. It begins with an overview of the Python programming language and introduces tools such as the Pandas library, integrated development environments (IDEs), Jupyter notebooks, and application programming interfaces (APIs) for accessing LLMs. A second section provides a hands-on guide for setting up a computer environment, with step-by-step code examples designed to familiarize readers with NLP libraries and LLMs. It emphasizes the acquisition of programming skills to better adapt and utilize LLM capabilities for qualitative data analysis while providing multiple resources for further learning.

Keywords Programming tools · Large language models

This chapter consists of two sections. The first section introduces the systems and tools that researchers can use to leverage NLP and LLMs in qualitative research, with a focus on accessibility for noncoders. It contains an overview of the Python programming language, followed by descriptions of Pandas (a widely used data processing library), integrated development environments (IDEs), Jupyter notebooks, and application programming interfaces (APIs) used to access LLMs. The second section

© The Author(s) 2026
D. Garcia Quevedo and J. Kuri, *AI for Qualitative Research*,
https://doi.org/10.1007/978-3-032-08872-7_5

describes how to set up a computer to use these tools and provides code examples with step-by-step instructions on how to use NLP libraries and LLMs in qualitative research.

The systems, tools, and techniques described in this chapter may be unfamiliar to readers without a computer programming background. To help you learn effectively, we adopted a hands-on approach, progressing from simple to more elaborate code examples of how to use LLMs in qualitative research and explaining important programming concepts along the way. The intention is not to teach programming (for which there are numerous online resources) but to give researchers enough examples that they can understand and later adapt to their needs. For example, once you understand the code provided in Chapter 8 for a technique called zero-shot classification, you can replace the sample data with your own data and adapt the provided model prompts to your needs.

Beyond the initial examples, acquiring programming skills becomes critical to fully realize the benefits and address the limitations of LLMs. For example, evaluating the quality of classification, topic modeling, or information retrieval results produced by different LLMs, or evaluating the variability of results across multiple executions of a model. More importantly, models are rapidly improving and offering an expanding array of capabilities. The fastest and most effective way to use these capabilities in creative ways to address research questions is through computer programs that access the models through their APIs. Acquiring this knowledge is an investment that significantly increases the productivity and analytical capabilities of researchers.

In this chapter, we provide links to various websites where you can find additional information on the concepts and resources presented. These external sources provide detailed information and examples that are useful for beginners.

LEARNING THE BASICS

Python Programming Language

Python is a versatile, high-level programming language used across data science, machine learning (ML), NLP, and other fields. Known for its simple and readable syntax, Python allows users to focus on solving their problems rather than dealing with complex language mechanics. This accessibility has made Python a preferred choice for researchers with limited coding experience who seek to integrate computational methods into their work.

The popularity of Python stems from its ease of learning and use, extensive library ecosystem, cross-platform compatibility, and strong community support. Python is concise and easy to read, offering a rich collection of libraries and frameworks such as Pandas and NumPy for data analysis and Scikit-learn and TensorFlow for machine learning model development. Popular NLP libraries include spaCy, NLTK, and Hugging-Face Transformers. Python runs on macOS, Windows, and Linux, which ensures accessibility and flexibility. Finally, the language has a vast, active community that continually develops resources, tutorials, and forums to help learners and practitioners troubleshoot issues and enhance their skills.

ML practitioners favor Python because of its integration with ML tools, support for data processing, and wide adoption in research. These developments have made Python a commonly used language for interacting with LLMs. The language is integrated with popular frameworks such as TensorFlow, PyTorch, and HuggingFace, making it easy to develop, train, and deploy models. Tools such as Dask help handle large datasets efficiently, whereas libraries such as Matplotlib and Seaborn can be used to create data visualizations. Python is widely used across academia and industry, which makes it easier to access shared datasets, pretrained models, and collaborative tools.

There are several excellent online resources where beginners can learn Python. The official Python website, Python.org, offers comprehensive documentation and tutorials. For more interactive learning, Codecademy and DataCamp provide platforms focused on Python basics and their applications in data science and machine learning. Additionally, Kaggle is a great resource that not only hosts data science competitions but also offers free Python tutorials and datasets for hands-on practice. Finally, YouTube channels such as Corey Schafer and freeCodeCamp.org provide detailed video tutorials on Python and its various libraries.

If you are new to programming, we recommend visiting one of the resources above to set up your computer to start working with Python.

Pandas Library

Pandas is an open-source Python library widely used in data science for data manipulation and analysis. The library provides tools that simplify working with large, structured datasets. There are two main data structures in Pandas: Series and DataFrame. The first is a one-dimensional labeled array, such as a list of numbers, each with another associated attribute, such as date or name. A DataFrame is a two-dimensional table with labeled rows and columns. Pandas provides functions for data manipulation (e.g., add/delete/modify rows or columns, filter/sort/group data), data analysis (e.g., aggregate and summarize, analyze trends in time series), data cleaning (e.g., handle missing or duplicate data), and integration (e.g., read/write various data formats, preprocess data for machine learning or visualization). Throughout the examples, we use the Pandas library to facilitate the manipulation and processing of the 1115 posts that comprise the synthetic dataset provided with the book.

Integrated Development Environments

An integrated development environment (IDE) is a software application that provides a set of tools to write, test, and debug code efficiently. IDEs integrate a code editor, a language compiler or interpreter, a terminal to run commands, project management tools, support version control, and other features to streamline the coding process and increase productivity. IDEs are helpful for beginners because they detect errors early and offer learning aids such as code suggestions, autocomplete tutorials, and built-in tutorials. Two popular IDEs for Python are PyCharm and Visual Studio Code (VS Code). Cloud-based IDEs include Replit, CodeSandbox, and GitHub Codespaces.

Coding Assistants and Agents

Beyond human language tasks, LLMs are used effectively as AI coding assistants since programming languages have simpler grammar than human languages do, and there are large repositories of high-quality source code that can be used for training. AI coding assistants perform tasks such as code completion, error detection and debugging, code refactoring, code documentation, automated testing, and language translation. These assistants improve productivity, increase accessibility for nonexperts, enhance collaboration—owing to improved code readability and documentation—and enable rapid prototyping of new ideas. These systems, however, have limitations and risks, such as generating erroneous code, creating overreliance, and inadvertently introducing security vulnerabilities. Erroneous code can range from simple syntax errors to complex issues such as logic that does not achieve the intended goal or code that references nonexistent libraries. Overreliance can occur for users with limited or no coding experience, who may fail to critically review the generated code, building fragile systems that they do not fully understand. Security vulnerabilities include memory safety bugs, hard-coded secrets, or improper input validations.

AI coding assistants are rapidly evolving with four main types currently available: Web-based AI development tools, IDE extensions, stand-alone AI-first IDEs, and command line interface (CLI) agents. Examples of web-based AI tools include Google AI Studio and Firebase Studio. Two popular extensions to VS Code include GitHub Copilot, cline.bot, and Roo. Stand-alone AI-first IDEs include Cursor and Windsurf. Finally, CLI agent coding tools include Anthropic's Claude Code and OpenAI's Codex CLI. For those interested in knowing more about coding assistants, the blog post "Comparing Modern AI Coding Assistants," by R. Infante, provides a comprehensive presentation.

These tools are rapidly evolving from passive coding assistants to advanced agentic software development systems that act as active collaborators. The systems can take user instructions in natural language, automatically generate a plan, execute commands, edit multiple files, and perform other functions to achieve the goal.

Early experience with coding assistants and agents indicates that it remains important for beginners to learn computer programming rather than unquestioningly trusting the output of the coding assistant. Paradoxically, users who have developed sound programming skills benefit the most from these systems.

Jupyter Notebooks

Jupyter notebooks are not an IDE but rather a type of document for interactive computing widely adopted in data science, ML, and research because of its ease of use. Key features include interactive code execution, support for multiple programming languages, rich text formatting, integrated data visualizations, and export/sharing options. Notebooks with Python code are usually stored in files with a.ipynb extension, which stands for the "interactive Python notebook." The notebooks can be developed and edited in stand-alone systems such as JupyterLab, in IDEs such as VS Code, or in cloud-based ML platforms.

Application Programming Interfaces (APIs)

An application programming interface (API) is a set of rules, protocols, and tools that allows different software applications or components to communicate with each other. It defines how requests and responses are formatted, enabling developers to interact with external systems, services, or libraries without needing to understand their internal workings. This simplification fosters innovation, accelerates development, and allows users to create complex systems by leveraging existing services and data sources. Examples of APIs include the Pandas library API and the APIs used to interact with LLMs. The LLMs can be hosted either locally on a computer or online, as in the case of OpenAI's GPT, Anthropic's Claude, Google's Gemini, or xAI's Grok.

GETTING HANDS-ON

Setting Up Your Development Environment

This book uses Jupyter notebooks to teach you how to use LLMs since they are easy to use. Interactive notebooks help beginners quickly grasp concepts and experiment with code. We recommend setting up your own local development environment to easily use the provided code and datasets.

To get started, follow these steps. We provide external links to help you set up your programming environment:

1. Install Visual Studio Code (VS Code https://code.visualstudio. com/).
2. Install Python3. We recommend the Anaconda Python distribution, as it is widely used and comes with many necessary packages preinstalled. The detailed installation instructions are available at Getting Started with Python in VS Code (https://code.visualstudio.com/ docs/python/python-tutorial).
3. Install the VS Code Jupyter extension at https://marketplace.visual studio.com/items?itemName=ms-toolsai.jupyter to develop notebooks directly in VS Code.
4. Follow the Jupyter Notebooks in VS Code (https://code.visual studio.com/docs/datascience/jupyter-notebooks) tutorial to learn how to navigate and interact with notebooks in this environment.

5. Create a new directory named `ai_for_qualitative_` `analysis` and copy into it the content of the Diana-GQ/ai_ for_qualitative_analysis repository (https://github.com/Diana-GQ/ai_for_qualitative_analysis). You can do this manually, using either the `git` command or the GitHub Desktop application (https://github.com/apps/desktop).
6. Launch VS Code to access the sample code. From the "File" menu, click on "Open Folder..." and select the directory created in the previous step.

When libraries are not available by default in your Python installation, you need to install them with a package manager such as `pip3` or `conda`, which is part of the Anaconda distribution. In the following subsections, we use `pip3` since it is widely used and not specific to a Python distribution.

The Diana-GQ/ai_for_qualitative_analysis repository is organized into four directories: `data`, `notebooks`, `html_docs`, and`scripts`. The `data` directory contains text files with synthetic social media posts in comma-separated-values format (files with extension `.csv`). It also contains image files used in the image classification example explained below. The `notebooks` directory contains the Jupyter notebooks with the code examples used throughout the rest of the book (files with extension `.ipynb`). For each notebook, the `html_docs` directory contains a web page with an LLM-generated explanation of the code in the notebook (files with extension `.html`). These files can be opened with a web browser. Finally, the `scripts` directory contains a collection of Python scripts (files with extension `.py`) from which the notebooks and HTML files were generated. For example, the `scripts/translation_hf.py` script was used to generate the corresponding `notebooks/translation_hf.ipynb` and `html_docs/` `translation_hf.html` files. You can rely solely on the notebooks to understand the examples presented throughout the book. The scripts are included in the repository only for completeness.

Accessing APIs for a Variety of Projects

The following subsections provide code examples and step-by-step instructions on how to use the HuggingFace, OpenAI, Groq, and Gemini models through their APIs. We provide a variety of examples to help you understand how they can evaluate and choose the model(s) best suited for their research needs. This is important, as there are differences in capabilities, performance, and cost across the available models, and these differences evolve over time. The examples also introduce the specific Python coding style that will be used in the following chapters. The goal of these examples is to provide foundational programming knowledge that will be used when leveraging LLMs to perform multiple NLP tasks.

How to Use the HuggingFace API

Hugging Face is a popular open-source platform for NLP and ML. The platform is known for its transformers library, which provides easy-to-use pretrained models for tasks such as text generation, translation, and sentiment analysis.

The goal of this section is to explain how to access the HuggingFace API. We do this through a code example that translates a given text from French to English. The code is available in the `translation_ hf.ipynb` notebook. We provide a high-level and line-by-line description of the code. In addition, an LLM-generated description is available in the `translation_hf.html` file. While this may seem redundant, a human-generated explanation is important since LLM-generated descriptions may overlook details important to readers unfamiliar with programming concepts. The LLM-generated descriptions are provided to showcase another use of LLMs as a complementary learning resource. With varied resources, you can decide what works best for you.

The first step involves installing the `transformers` and `torch` libraries needed by the code via the following command:

```
pip3 install transformers torch
```

Torch is an open-source machine learning framework developed by Meta that the Transformers library uses.

At a high level, the code below defines a variable `source_text` containing the text to be translated, calls a pretrained model to perform the translation, retrieves the result, and displays it in an easy-to-read manner.

```
1:     from transformers import pipeline
2:     # Set the text to translate
3:     source_text = (
4:         "Dans les champs de l'observation, le hasard ne
       favorise "
5:         "que les esprits préparés."
6:     )
7:
8:     # Select a translation model for French-to-English
9:     # https://huggingface.co/Helsinki-NLP/opus-mt-fr-en
10:    translation_model = "Helsinki-NLP/opus-mt-fr-en"
11:
12:    # Create the translation task
13:    translator = pipeline("translation", model=translation_
       model)
14:
15:    # Execute the translation
16:    # Results is a list of dictionaries with the translated
       text.
17:    result = translator(source_text)
18:
19:    # Display the original and translated text
20:    print(f"Source text: {source_text}")
21:    print(f"Translated text: {result[0]['translation_
       text']}")
```

Line 1 imports the `pipeline` function from the `transformers` library.

Lines starting with the "#" symbol (e.g., lines 2, 8, and 9) are comments used to document the code. They are ignored by Python when the code is executed. These comments are important, as they provide a brief explanation of the code for human readers, making it easier to understand and outlining the process of the code.

Lines 3 to 6 define a variable named `source_text` containing the text to be translated. The text to be translated is written using two lines each between quotation marks ("text"). This is an example of Python's implicit string concatenation. When two or more strings of text are placed next to each other, separated only by spaces, Python automatically joins them into a single string. The technique is often used to break long lines into more readable segments.

Line 10 assigns the `"Helsinki-NLP/opus-mt-fr-en"` string to the `translation_model` variable, specifying the pretrained translation model to be used. Line 13 initializes a translation pipeline. It calls the imported pipeline function, specifying `"translation"` as the task and passing the chosen `translation_model`. This creates a translator object capable of performing French-to-English translation.

Line 17 executes the translation. The translator pipeline instance, instantiated in line 13, is called directly with the `source_text` as its argument. The pipeline processes the text via the loaded model and returns the translation. The output is typically a list of Python dictionaries. A list is a Python data structure that stores a collection of items. The items have a defined order and can be of different types. For example, [1, 2, 3, 4], ["apple", "banana", "cherry"], and [10, "hello", 3.14, True] are all valid lists. In the Python syntax, lists are delimited by square brackets. A dictionary in Python is a collection of data in which each item consists of a key and a value. The key is used to look up, retrieve, and update the value. A dictionary can be used, for example, to store three pieces of information about a person: {"name": "Alice", "age": 30, "city": "New York"}. A list of dictionaries can thus be used to store the records of different people. More information about the Python data structures is available online at https://docs.python.org/3/tutorial/datastructures.html.

Lines 20 and 21 display the results. The first line displays the original French text. An f-string is used for easy formatting, displaying the label `"Source text:"` followed by the content of the `source_text` variable. F-strings, or formatted string literals, is a feature that provides a concise and readable way to embed Python expressions inside string literals. This feature is used extensively in the code examples of this book. For a detailed explanation, please consult https://docs.python.org/3/reference/lexical_analysis.html#f-strings. Line 21 prints the translated English text. Since the `result` variable (from line 17) is a list of dictionaries (even for a single input string), `result[0]` accesses the first (and only one) dictionary in the list. From this `result[0]` dictionary, `['translation_text']` extracts the actual translated string, which is then displayed with a prefix `"Translated text:"`. Figure 5.1 shows the output.

The following code is another example of using the HuggingFace API, but this time, it performs an image classification task. This example aims

> Source text: Dans les champs de l'observation, le hasard ne favorise que les esprits préparés.
>
> Translated text: In the fields of observation, chance only favours prepared minds.

Fig. 5.1 AI-generated output created with the Transformers library, Helsinki-NLP/opus-mt-fr-en, 2025, from the translation_hf.ipynb notebook

to familiarize you with the common code when calling pretrained functions, the use of stored files, in this case, an image, and the presentation of results via a loop.

The code is available in the `image_classification_hf.ipynb` notebook and the `image_classification_hf.py` script. An LLM-generated description of the code is available in the `image_classification_hf.html` file.

```
1:     # Import libraries
2:     from PIL import Image
3:     from transformers import pipeline
4:
5:     # Load the image to classify
6:     img = Image.open("../data/animal_
       image.jpeg")
7:
8:     # Select the classification model
9:     # https://huggingface.co/google/vit-base-
       patch16-224
10:    classification_model = "google/
       vit-base-patch16-224"
11:
12:    # Create the image classification task
13:    image_classifier = pipeline(
14:        "image-classification",
15:        model=classification_model,
16:    )
17:
18:    # Execute the task
19:    # result is a list of dictionaries, each
       with a label and a score.
20:    result = image_classifier(img)
21:
22:    # Display the results
23:    print("Image Classification Results:")
24:    for item in result:
```

(continued)

(continued)

25:	`print(f"Label: {item['label']}, Score: {item['score']:.4f}")`

As with the previous example and all the subsequent examples, each code starts with the import of libraries. Lines 2 and 3 import the `Image` and `pipeline` functions from the `PIL` and `transformers` libraries, respectively.

In this example, we introduce the code to upload a file located in a relative path. Line 6 uses the Image.open() function to load an image file named `animal_image.jpeg` from the specified relative path `"../data/"`. This is the location of the image file *relative* to where the notebook or script is executed. The `".."` string represents one level up in the directory hierarchy. For example, if the full path to the notebook is `"/Users/my_alias/Documents/GitHub/ai_for_qualitative_analysis/notebooks/image_classification_hf.ipynb"`, the `"../data/animal_image.jpeg"` relative path refers to the `"/Users/my_alias/Documents/GitHub/ai_for_qualitative_analysis/data/animal_image.jpeg"` file. The opened image object is then assigned to the variable img.

Lines 10 to 20 share the same structure as in the previous example. First, the model is selected; second, a task is created via the pipeline function; and finally, the task is executed. Line 10 stores the name of the pretrained image classification model in the `classification_model` variable. The specific model chosen here is Google's Vision Transformer (ViT). The code in lines 13 to 16 sets up the process for classifying images. It selects the task ("image classification") and the model to be used. This creates an image classifier object capable of classifying an image into a predefined category and providing its score. This entire setup is then assigned to the `image_classifier` variable.

Line 20 executes the image classification task. The image classifier processes the image via the selected model. It returns a list of Python dictionaries, where each dictionary contains a predicted 'label' and its corresponding 'score' (confidence), ordered by confidence. This list of results is stored in the `result` variable.

Lines 23 to 25 display the results. In this example, the results contain the classification and the confidence score. To display the results, line 24 initiates a `for` loop that iterates through each Python dictionary within

Fig. 5.2 AI-generated
output created with the
Transformers library,
google/
vit-base-patch16-224,
2025, from the image_
classification_hf.ipynb
notebook

Image Classification Results:
Label: Egyptian cat, Score: 0.5144
Label: tabby, tabby cat, Score: 0.1930
Label: tiger cat, Score: 0.0683
Label: lynx, catamount, Score: 0.0563
Label: weasel, Score: 0.0307

the `result` list. Each dictionary represents a single classification prediction (e.g., 'dog' with a specific score). Line 25 uses a formatted string (f-string) to print the label and score for the current classification item in the loop; `item['label']` and `item['score']` access the label and score values, respectively. The `":.4f"` format specifier ensures that the score is displayed as a number with four decimal places. The output is shown in Fig. 5.2.

The previous examples are based on pretrained LLMs of free access. In the following sections, we explain the use of paid service APIs such as OpenAI and Google. Although LLM providers offer free platforms to access their models, such as ChatGPT and Gemini, we recommend using paid service APIs for two key reasons. First, paid service warrants the confidentiality of the data sent to the LLM. OpenAI and Google both specify in their terms of service that the data processed through their paid service will not be used for training purposes and will be deleted after processing. This is not the case for their free services. Second, APIs allow flexibility in processing and analyzing data. Although prompts can be run easily through online platforms, data handling and organization become easier when they are combined with commonly used Python libraries such as Pandas. As such, all the examples presented in the book used a paid API service combined with Python functions.

How to Use the OpenAI API

The first step in using the OpenAI API is to install the `openai` Python library via the following command:

```
pip3 install openai
```

The library was initially developed to access the OpenAI API. However, since it is widely used, it has become a de facto standard and can also be used to access APIs from other providers, such as Groq and Google Gemini, by changing a few lines of code.

To get started with the OpenAI API, go to platform.openai.com and create an account. Since OpenAI models are offered as paid services, payment information, such as credit card numbers, needs to be entered. Once logged into your account, go to the quickstart page and follow the instructions to create an API key. The API key is a text string used as a code to access the models through the API. The key must be kept secret since the API usage associated with the key is billed to your account. We will use *environment variables* to achieve this. The variables are values set in the operating system (e.g., Windows, macOS, Linux), outside a program's code, to influence how the program behaves. They are primarily used to separate sensitive information from code and adapt application behavior to different environments.

For the notebooks and scripts in this book that require API keys to work, one needs to create a file named .env in the directory containing the code. In our case, a file with the following path is used: "/Users/my_alias/Documents/GitHub/ai_for_qualitative_analysis/.env". You can create and save this file with VS Code. The content of the file must look like the following:

```
OPENAI_API_KEY=tn-mt9X4s8pxB8NoWl5pwngQ5H9gpeYVPhsWCTcMwHXWG73
GROQ_API_KEY=mtf_F8DhL5TSmtCu5uf6oatfBW95MEH5emZJFwUe8PEenGQVDr
GEMINI_API_KEY=TWmiRcTWkUpxrfBmeWSa35F-nDe3065w93cG7Ee
HF_TOKEN=hf_MUidTGdTpwmuTRfeutgWNbytCnHQCTGHY2
```

There is one entry per line in the file. Each entry consists of the name of the key, the equal sign ("="), and the value of the key. The key values shown above are fictitious and used only to show the format of the file. The .env file is used by the load_dotenv function described below.

The following code illustrates how to use the OpenAI API. It is available in the example_openai_api.ipynb notebook. An LLM-generated description of the code is available in the example_openai_api.html file.

```
1:    # Import libraries
2:    import os
3:    from openai import OpenAI
4:    from dotenv import load_dotenv
5:
6:    def generate_llm_prompts():
7:        system_prompt = "You are a helpful assistant."
8:        user_prompt = "How does AI work?"
9:        messages = [
10:           {"role": "system", "content": system_prompt},
11:           {"role": "user", "content": user_prompt},
12:       ]
13:       return messages
14:
15:   # Load environment variables from .env file
16:   load_dotenv()
17:
18:   # Retrieve OpenAI API key from environment variable
19:   api_key = os.getenv("OPENAI_API_KEY")
20:   if not api_key:
21:       raise ValueError(
22:           "OPENAI_API_KEY not found in environment variables
      or .env file"
23:       )
24:
25:   # Initialize OpenAI client
26:   client = OpenAI(api_key=api_key)
27:
28:   # Select the model to use
29:   model = "gpt-4o-mini"
30:
31:   # Generate system and user prompts for the LLM
32:   prompts = generate_llm_prompts()
33:
34:   # Send the prompts to the OpenAI GPT model and get response
35:   result = client.chat.completions.create(model=model,
      messages=prompts)
36:
37:   # Print the model's response
38:   print(result.choices[0].message.content)
```

Lines 2 to 4 import all the necessary libraries. This example introduces the os library, which is used to access environment variables.

Lines 6 to 13 define a function called `generate_llm_prompts` to generate a prompt in the format expected by the API. Functions are blocks of code used to make a program modular and maintainable. A function can have input parameters and return values. In this case, the `generate_llm_prompts` function does not have input parameters but returns the prompt expected by the API. Inside the function, the `system_prompt` variable is assigned a string with instructions for the model's role or behavior. The `user_prompt` variable is assigned a string with the specific query that the user wants to send to the model. In this case, the question is `"How does AI work?"`.

Lines 9 to 12 create a list named `messages`. The list contains Python dictionaries, where each dictionary represents a message in the conversation. The OpenAI chat completion API expects prompts in this format, with each message having a "role" (e.g., "system", "user") and "content" (the actual text).

Line 13 returns the constructed list of messages, which will then be passed to the OpenAI API call.

Line 16 calls the `load_dotenv()` function, which loads the environment variables from the `.env` file described above.

Line 19 attempts to retrieve the value of the `OPENAI_API_KEY` environment variable and assign it to the `api_key` variable.

Lines 20 to 23 check whether the `api_key` variable exists. If it does not, it returns an error message.

Line 26 initializes the OpenAI client. It uses the `api_key` to ensure that the communication with the service is authorized.

Line 29 defines `"gpt-4o-mini"` as the model to be used in the API call. We recommend visiting platform.openai.com/docs/models for the list of currently available models.

Line 32 calls the previously defined function `generate_llm_prompts` to generate the list of formatted messages (system and user prompts) and stores the result in the `prompts` variable.

Line 35 makes the call to the OpenAI API. The `client.chat.completions.create()` method is used to request a chat-based completion from the model. This is the main OpenAI API function used throughout the book to generate text from prompts. We recommend reviewing the complete documentation at platform.openai. com/docs/api-reference/chat/create. In this call, we only pass the two required parameters, `model` and `messages`, but there is a long list of optional parameters that can also be passed to control the behavior of the model. In particular, the `temperature` (default to 1) and `top_p` (default to 1) parameters, explained in Chapter 2, control the randomness in the produced output. In the API, the `temperature` parameter accepts values between 0 and 2, and the `top_p` parameter values are greater than 0 and up to 1. The response from the API call is stored in the `result` variable.

Line 38 prints the response from the model. The API response often contains a list of completion choices; `result.choices[0]` selects the first choice from the list; `.message` accesses the message object within that choice; and `.content` retrieves the actual text content generated by the LLM in response to the prompts. The OpenAI API documentation mentioned above contains detailed examples of the complete response from the call to the model.

Figure 5.3 shows a brief sample of the possible outputs from the model. Since LLMs are probabilistic, the text that you obtain by running the script may be different from the one shown here.

To learn more, OpenAI quickstart guide provides an introduction and sample code of how to use the GPT models for text generation, image generation, embedding generation, text-to-speech, speech-to-text generation, and other tasks.

Artificial Intelligence (AI) works through a combination of algorithms, data, and computing power to perform tasks that typically require human intelligence. Here's a high-level overview of how AI functions:

1. **Data Collection and Preparation**: AI systems require large amounts of data to learn from. This data can be text, images, videos, or any other type of information. The data is often cleaned and preprocessed to ensure that it is suitable for analysis. This step might involve removing noise, dealing with missing values, and converting data into a format that a computer can understand.

2. **Machine Learning Algorithms**: At the core of many AI systems are machine learning algorithms. These algorithms learn patterns from the data. Common types of machine learning include:

   - **Supervised Learning**: The model is trained on labeled data, where the outcome is known. The algorithm learns to predict the labels for new, unseen data.
   - **Unsupervised Learning**: The model is trained on unlabeled data and tries to identify patterns or groupings within the data.
   - **Reinforcement Learning**: The algorithm learns by interacting with an environment and receiving feedback in the form of rewards or penalties.

Fig. 5.3 AI-generated output created with OpenAI API, GPT-4o-mini, 2025, from the example_openai_api.ipynb notebook

How to Use the Groq API

Groq (not to be confused with the Grok LLM from xAI) is a start-up developing hardware for accelerated AI inference. The company also hosts a collection of open-weight LLMs accessible through an API. The list of hosted models is available at console.groq.com/docs/models. Currently, it includes Llama from Meta, GPT-OSS from OpenAI, Gemma from Google, DeepSeek, and Qwen from the Alibaba Cloud. The API makes it easy for users to evaluate the outputs from multiple models and select the one that best fits their needs. This is an important feature for obtaining the most from a dynamic LLM ecosystem in which model capabilities evolve rapidly.

The first step in using the Groq API is to install the groq Python library via the following command:

```
pip3 install groq
```

To start with the API, go to console.groq.com and create an account. Once logged into the account, go to console.groq.com/keys and follow the instructions to create an API key. Then, add the key, with the name GROQ_API_KEY, to the .env file described in the previous subsection.

The following code is available in the example_groq_api.ipynb notebook. An LLM-generated description of the code is available in the example_groq_api.html file.

```
1:    # Import libraries
2:    import os
3:    from groq import Groq
4:    from dotenv import load_dotenv
5:
6:    def generate_llm_prompts():
7:        system_prompt = "You are a helpful assistant."
8:        user_prompt = "How does AI work?"
9:        messages = [
10:           {"role": "system", "content": system_prompt},
11:           {"role": "user", "content": user_prompt},
12:        ]
13:        return messages
14:
15:    # Load environment variables from .env file
16:    load_dotenv()
17:
```

(continued)

(continued)

```
18:      # Retrieve Groq API key from environment variable
19:      api_key = os.getenv("GROQ_API_KEY")
20:      if not api_key:
21:          raise ValueError(
22:              "GROQ_API_KEY not found in environment variables
         or .env file"
23:          )
24:
25:      # Initialize Groq client
26:      client = Groq(api_key=api_key)
27:
28:      # Set the list of models in Groq to use (June 2025)
29:      models_in_groq = [
30:          "gemma2-9b-it",
31:          "openai/gpt-oss-20b",
32:          "llama-3.3-70b-versatile",
33:          "qwen/qwen3-32b"
34:      ]
35:
36:      # Generate system and user prompts for the LLM
37:      prompts = generate_llm_prompts()
38:
39:      for model in models_in_groq:
40:          # Send the prompts to each model and get response
41:          result = client.chat.completions.create(model=model,
         messages=prompts)
42:          # Print the model's response
43:          print(f"\n\n >>> Response from model '{model}':\n\n")
44:          print(result.choices[0].message.content)
```

Lines 1 to 26 are the same as in the OpenAI API example, except that the Groq library and API key are used instead of the OpenAI equivalents.

Lines 29 to 34 create a Python list named models_in_groq. This list contains strings identifying different LLM models available via the Groq API. The list needs to be updated with models currently hosted in the platform (console.groq.com/docs/models).

Line 37 calls the generate_llm_prompts function and assigns its returned list of messages to the prompts variable.

Lines 39 to 44 implement a loop that sends the prompts to each model in the models_in_groq list and prints its response. In each iteration, an item from the list is assigned to the model variable.

```
>>> Response from model 'llama-3.3-70b-versatile':
```

Introduction to AI

Artificial Intelligence (AI) refers to the development of computer systems that can perform tasks that would typically require human intelligence, such as learning, problem-solving, decision-making, and perception. AI systems use algorithms and data to make predictions, classify objects, and generate insights.

Key Components of AI

1. **Machine Learning (ML):** A subset of AI that involves training algorithms on data to enable them to learn from experience and improve their performance over time.
2. **Deep Learning (DL):** A type of ML that uses neural networks to analyze data and make predictions.
3. **Natural Language Processing (NLP):** A field of AI that deals with the interaction between computers and humans in natural language.
4. **Computer Vision:** A field of AI that enables computers to interpret and understand visual data from images and videos.

Fig. 5.4 AI-generated output created with Groq API, Llama-3.3-70b-versatile, 2025, from the example_groq_api.ipynb notebook

Line 41 uses the client initialized in line 26 to make a call to the API with the value of the `model` and `prompts` variables as input parameters. If needed, optional parameters such as `temperature` or `top_p`, with the same meaning as in the OpenAI API, can be added to this API call.

Line 43 prints a formatted string (f-string) indicating which model's response is about to be displayed. The `"\n\n"` at the beginning of the string adds two new lines for better readability between model outputs.

Line 44 extracts and prints the actual text content of the LLM's response.

Figure 5.4 shows a brief sample of the possible outputs from the models. Since LLMs are probabilistic, the text that you obtain by running the script may be different from the one shown here.

How to Use the Google Gemini API

The first step in using the Gemini API is to install the `genai` Python library via the following command:

```
pip3 install genai
```

Alternatively, the `openai` Python library introduced above can be used to access the Gemini API by setting the `base_url` parameter in the OpenAI() client instantiation function to https://generativelanguage. googleapis.com/v1beta/openai/:

```
client = openai. OpenAI(
base_url="  https://generativelanguage.googleapis.com/v1beta/
openai/",
api_key=os.environ.get("GEMINI_API_KEY")
)
```

To start with the API, go to aistudio.google.com/app/apikey. If prompted, log in with a Google account. Then click on the "Create API key" button and follow the instructions. Once you obtain the key, add it to the `.env` file described before with the name `GEMINI_API_KEY`.

The following code performs a more complex task of using an LLM to explain in detail what a small block of Python code does. The idea is to create a prompt containing the code to be explained, as well as specific instructions on how to produce the explanation. We use a similar approach in the following chapters for other tasks. An extended version of LLM-generated code explanations is implemented in the `utils/ python_to_html.py` script available in the GitHub repository. The code explained below is available in the `example_gemini_api.ipynb` notebook. An LLM-generated description of the code is available in the `example_gemini_api.html` file.

```
1:    # Import libraries
2:    import os
3:    from google import genai
4:    from dotenv import load_dotenv
5:    from IPython.display import display, HTML
6:    from datetime import datetime, timezone
7:
8:    # Load environment variables from .env file
9:    load_dotenv()
10:
11:   # Retrieve Gemini API key from environment variable
12:   api_key = os.getenv("GEMINI_API_KEY")
13:   if not api_key:
14:       raise ValueError(
```

(continued)

(continued)

```
15:              "GEMINI_API_KEY not found in environment variables
       or .env file."
16:       )
17:
18:    # Initialize Gemini client
19:    client = genai.Client(api_key=api_key)
20:
21:    # Set the model to use
22:    model = "gemini-2.5-flash"
23:
24:    # Get current UTC date and time
25:    current_time =
       datetime.now(timezone.utc).strftime("%Y-%m-%d %H:%M:%S
       UTC")
26:
27:    # Set the user prompt
28:    prompt = f"""
29:        Explain the following code snippet in detail.
30:        Refer to the line numbers in the explanation.
31:        Include the following line at the beginning of the
       explanation:
32:        "This code explanation was generated with {model} on
       {current_time}."
33:        Do not include the code snippet itself in the
       explanation.
34:        Produce the output in HTML format.
35:
36:        # Import libraries
37:        import os
38:        from google import genai
39:        from dotenv import load_dotenv
40:
41:        # Load environment variables from .env file
42:        load_dotenv()
43:
44:        # Retrieve Gemini API key from environment variable
45:        api_key = os.getenv("GEMINI_API_KEY")
46:        if not api_key:
47:            raise ValueError(
48:                "GEMINI_API_KEY not found in environment
       variables."
49:            )
50:
51:        # Initialize Gemini client
```

(continued)

(continued)

```
52:        client = genai.Client(api_key=api_key)
53:
54:
55:        model = "gemini-2.5-flash"
56:
57:        prompt = "How does AI work?"
58:
59:           response = client.models.generate_content(model=model,
           contents=prompt)
60:
61:           print(response.text)
62:    """
63:
64:    # Send the prompt to the Gemini model and get response
65:    response = client.models.generate_content(model=model,
           contents=prompt)
66:
67:    # Display the response in HTML format
68:    display(HTML(response.text))
```

Like in the previous notebooks, lines 2 to 22 import libraries and functions, load the environment variables from the .env file, instantiate a client to communicate with the LLM through the API, and assign to the model variable a string with the name of the model to use.

Line 25 obtains the current date and time in UTC (Coordinated Universal Time) using datetime.now(timezone.utc), formats the output with the strftime function to produce a string such as "2025–08-17 12:53:09 UTC", and assigns that string to the current_time variable.

Line 28 defines a multiline-formatted string (f-string) that serves as the input request (prompt) to the Gemini model. In line 32, the values of the model and current_time variables are inserted into the prompt. For example, if the values of the variables are "gemini-2.5-flash" and "2025–08-17 12:53:09 UTC", the content of the prompt will be (truncated for brevity):

```
f"""
    Explain the following code snippet in detail.
    Refer to the line numbers in the explanation.
```

```
        Include  the  following  line  at  the  beginning  of  the
explanation:
        "This code explanation was generated with gemini-2.5-flash
on 2025-08-17 12:53:09 UTC."
        Do not include the code snippet itself in the explanation.
        Produce the output in HTML format.
        ...
"""
```

Lines 29 to 35, within the prompt, specify the instructions for the model. They direct the LLM to explain a code snippet in detail, refer to line numbers, include a specific introductory line (with the model's name and timestamp), avoid including the code snippet it explains, and produce the output in HTML format. Lines 36 to 61 contain the actual Python code that the LLM is instructed to explain. Importantly, this code is part of the prompt string and is not executed directly by the current script. Line 62 concludes the multiline f-string definition for the `prompt` variable.

Line 65 makes the call to the API with the two required parameters: `model` and `contents`. If needed, optional parameters such as `temperature` or `top-P` can be added to the function call, although the way this is done in the Gemini API is different than that in the OpenAI API. See ai.google.dev/api/generate-content#generationconfig for details. An illustration of how to use these parameters in the Gemini API is provided in the code implementing a retrieval-augmented generation (RAG) example in Chapter 10.

Line 68 applies the `HTML()` function from the `IPython` library imported in line 5 to convert the text in the LLM response, `response.text`, into a webpage format, which is then displayed in the notebook via the `display()` function. For example, of what the LLM-generated code explanations look like, open the files with extension `.html` in the `html_docs` directory of the GitHub repository with a web browser such as Chrome, Safari, or Firefox.

Once the Python environment has been created, the necessary libraries have been installed, and the APIs have been tested, we can start using these tools for data analysis. In the next chapter, we explain the method developed by Garcia Quevedo et al. (2025) and apply it in subsequent chapters.

REFERENCE

Garcia Quevedo, D., Glaser, A., & Verzat, C. (2025). Enhancing Theorization Using Artificial Intelligence: Leveraging Large Language Models for Qualitative Analysis of Online Data. Organizational Research Methods, 29(1), 92-112. https://doi.org/10.1177/10944281251339144

CHAPTER 6

Using LLMs in Qualitative Analysis

Abstract This chapter presents the method developed by Garcia Quevedo et al. in *Organizational Research Methods* (2025) for qualitative analysis of large, unstructured datasets using large language models (LLMs). It addresses the limitations of traditional random sampling by proposing a structured approach that efficiently explores and selects relevant data for manual analysis. The method integrates three natural language processing (NLP) tasks: sentiment analysis, topic modeling, and information retrieval, allowing for comprehensive dataset exploration and selection. These tasks are covered in the subsequent chapters.

Keywords Qualitative analysis · Natural language processing · Large language models

This chapter explains the method for qualitative analysis of large online datasets developed by Garcia Quevedo et al. (2025). The authors argued that the vastness and unstructured nature of online data have traditionally posed a significant barrier to qualitative researchers. Due to its nature, qualitative researchers have often resorted to random sampling when large online datasets are used to manage their size and complexity. However, randomizing imposes leaving data behind and diminishes the understanding of the entire dataset. The authors proposed a method

© The Author(s) 2026
D. Garcia Quevedo and J. Kuri, *AI for Qualitative Research*,
https://doi.org/10.1007/978-3-032-08872-7_6

leveraging LLMs to explore and select relevant data efficiently before manual inductive analysis.

A Method for Relevant Data Selection

Garcia Quevedo, Glaser, and Verzat's method combines various NLP tasks via LLM-based algorithms to analyze large unstructured datasets efficiently. This approach involves three key aspects: (1) exploring the entire dataset; (2) gaining a deep understanding of the dataset; and (3) creating a focused selection ready for manual inductive analysis. The method aims to create a small sample following a conscious, step-by-step selection procedure of relevant data through a deep exploration and understanding of the entire dataset, leveraging LLMs.

The method leverages classification and information retrieval techniques to explore and select relevant online data efficiently for inductive qualitative analysis. Therefore, the method integrates three NLP tasks via LLM algorithms: (1) sentiment analysis for classifying expressions via an affective tenor; (2) topic modeling for identifying underlying data patterns and clustering; and (3) information retrieval for finding similarities at the sentence and paragraph levels. This combined approach diversifies data exploration and enables triangulation during data selection. Furthermore, it facilitates conscious, step-by-step choices aligned with the research question, promoting efficient dataset exploration, understanding, and content utilization. By incorporating multiple NLP tasks, the method enables comprehensive dataset analysis.

The authors provide recommendations for applying the three NLP tasks as best practices when dealing with large unstructured datasets. Then, they applied a two-step method: (1) selection by category, including sentiment analysis and topic modeling, and (2) targeted search, including information retrieval via sentence similarity. They argue that this order will avoid confirmatory biases and the risk of circularity (Dana & Dumez, 2015), where the researcher's initial assumption influences the selection process. They claim that using diverse NLP tasks enables data triangulation during the selection process, thereby ensuring that the entire dataset is considered and that the selected data are the most relevant to the research question. The authors demonstrate that LLM-based algorithms prove effective in finding relevant data and facilitating the efficient analysis of large datasets. Once the relevant data selection had been completed, the authors conducted a manual inductive analysis on the selected data.

The method offers significant advantages for qualitative researchers. It provides great flexibility and adaptability for a variety of research projects. It enables the analysis of different sizes and types of data, including YouTube video transcripts, film scripts, and blogs. It allows for comprehensive coverage of the entire dataset by exploring the data from multiple perspectives through the three NLP tasks. Researchers can be confident that the selected data represent the most relevant information, enabling them to gain a deep understanding of the entire dataset. The method allows for the efficient utilization of time and resources. Thus, their method streamlines data analysis, saving time by automating parts of the research workflow and allowing for more efficient exploration and interpretation of the data.

IMPLEMENTING LLMS IN QUALITATIVE ANALYSIS

In the following chapters, we propose several approaches that use LLMs to identify patterns and relationships in text. However, we acknowledge that LLMs do not possess genuine interpretive capabilities or a human-like understanding (Rasheed et al., 2024; Schroeder et al., 2024). Only researchers can grasp the deeper meaning, nuances, and contextual factors that inform an interpretative qualitative analysis. Researchers could think of their LLM tools as "stochastic parrots" (Bender et al., 2021), which are able to mimic human language patterns without understanding the underlying meaning.

As we explain in the following chapters, implementing a qualitative analysis via LLMs requires a well-considered process of (1) choosing the correct model and its parameters; (2) crafting precise and comprehensive prompts; (3) comparing and validating outputs of various executions; and (4) critically evaluating the generated response. Additionally, we recommend documenting the multiple steps and decisions (e.g., choice of model and parameters) taken throughout the process to increase rigor and transparency in the analysis.

Garcia-Quevedo et al. (2025) focused on three NLP tasks: sentiment analysis for classification, topic modeling for clustering, and information retrieval for targeted search. In this book, we expand upon their work, including their recommendations for initial exploration leveraging LLMs, other forms of classification beyond sentiment analysis, and clustering via hierarchical topic modeling. We also expand on information retrieval (IR) by incorporating retrieval-augmented generation (RAG). The following chapters explain the algorithms and Python code for these tasks. Each chapter describes each task separately. Chapter 7 covers the code for initial exploratory analysis. Chapter 8 covers classification algorithms. Chapter 9 addresses clustering and topic modeling. Finally, Chapter 10 explores IR and RAG.

References

Bender, E. M., Gebru, T., McMillan-Major, A., & Shmitchell, S. (2021). On the dangers of stochastic parrots: Can language models be too big? *Proceedings of the 2021 ACM Conference on Fairness, Accountability, and Transparency*, 610–623. https://doi.org/10.1145/3442188.3445922

Dana, L. P., & Dumez, H. (2015). Qualitative research revisited: Epistemology of a comprehensive approach. *International Journal of Entrepreneurship and Small Business, 26*(2), 154–170. https://doi.org/10.1504/IJESB.2015.071822

Garcia Quevedo, D., Glaser, A., & Verzat, C. (2025). Enhancing theorization using artificial intelligence: Leveraging large language models for qualitative analysis of online data. *Organizational Research Methods, 29*(1), 92–112. https://doi.org/10.1177/10944281251339144

Rasheed, Z., Waseem, M., Ahmad, A., Kemell, K.-K., Xiaofeng, W., Duc, A. N., & Abrahamsson, P. (2024). *Can large language models serve as data analysts? A multi-agent assisted approach for qualitative data analysis* (No. arXiv:2402.01386). arXiv. https://doi.org/10.48550/arXiv.2402.01386

Schroeder, H., Quéré, M. A. L., Randazzo, C., Mimno, D., & Schoenebeck, S. (2024). *Large language models in qualitative research: Can we do the data justice?* (No. arXiv:2410.07362; Version 1). arXiv. https://doi.org/10.48550/arXiv.2410.07362

CHAPTER 7

Data Evaluation and Validation

Abstract This chapter provides code examples for data evaluation and validation, introducing two approaches: traditional coding and large language model-based approaches. This chapter provides a concrete example of the limitations of large language models (LLMs), particularly in terms of reliability for numerical tasks. Researchers are advised to critically evaluate LLM outputs and consider traditional programming techniques for tasks that require numerical accuracy.

Keywords Qualitative analysis · Data exploration · Large language models

Before launching a study involving large datasets, it is important to perform a thorough exploration of their content to identify gaps and determine their suitability for the study. This fundamental step is typically performed via the Pandas library and traditional NLP algorithms via the Natural Language Toolkit (NLTK) library. This chapter shows how to handle datasets and includes a brief demonstration of the limitations of LLMs, highlighting their stochastic nature. The chapter then provides avenues to mitigate these limitations.

The following code performs a brief exploration of the 1,115 synthetic social media posts. It demonstrates various functions of the Pandas library, including uploading a file and obtaining information about it. The code

D. Garcia Quevedo and J. Kuri, *AI for Qualitative Research*,
https://doi.org/10.1007/978-3-032-08872-7_7

displays the total number of columns and rows, column names, the first and last five rows, and the names of the fictitious personas. It is available in the `explore_dataframe.ipynb` notebook. An LLM-generated description of the code is available in the `explore_dataframe.html` file.

```
1:     import pandas as pd
2:     from IPython.display import display
3:     # Load the synthetic data CSV file
4:     df_synthetic_data = pd.read_csv("../data/All_Synthetic_
       Data.csv")
5:
6:     display(df_synthetic_data.info())
7:
8:     pd.set_option('display.max_colwidth', None)
9:
10:    display(df_synthetic_data.head())
11:    display(df_synthetic_data.tail())
12:
13:    display(df_synthetic_data['owner'].unique().tolist())
14:    display(df_synthetic_data['post_date'].aggregate(['min',
       'max']))
```

Lines 1 and 2 import the necessary libraries. In the first import, pd is used as an alias for the Pandas library. The `display` function is commonly used in interactive environments such as Jupyter notebooks to render rich outputs such as dataframes, images, and HTML code more effectively than with the standard `print()` statement.

Line 4 uses the Pandas `read_csv()` function to load the comma-separated-values (CSV) file `All_Synthetic_Data.csv` into a dataframe named `df_synthetic_data` from the specified relative path `"../data/"`. This is the location of the file *relative* to where the notebook or script is executed, similar to the example of the image classifier shown in Chapter 5.

Line 6 calls the `info()` method of the dataframe created in line 4, which prints a concise summary, including the number of entries, the number of columns, a list of all column names, their nonnull counts, and their data types. Identifying null entries is important since they correspond to missing data points. These entries can be replaced with default values, but if the fraction of missing values is greater than a threshold (defined by the researcher), the dataset may be unusable. The output of the `info()` method is then passed to the `display()` function for rendering in the notebook. The dataframe contains the following columns: `post_id`, `owner`, `post_date`, and `post_text`, as shown in Fig. 7.1.

Line 8 sets the `display.max_colwidth` global Pandas option to display the full content of the columns of a dataframe without truncation. This is useful when columns contain long strings.

Lines 10 and 11 display the first and last five rows in the dataframe. This provides a quick glimpse into the structure and content of the dataset. The `head()` and `tail()` methods display five rows by default, but a different number can be set.

Line 13 first selects the `'owner'` column from the dataframe. The `unique()` method is then applied to obtain all the unique values present in this column. Finally, the `tolist()` method converts the resulting unique values into a standard Python list.

Line 14 computes the range of dates in the `"post_date"` column by applying the `aggregate(['min', 'max'])` method to the column. Figure 7.1 shows the outputs of lines 10 to 11; for presentation purposes, these outputs have been truncated.

Additional information, such as the number of posts per owner or the distribution of post lengths (in words), can be generated to gain more insights into the dataset. Once we have a general understanding of the dataset, we can evaluate its content in more detail. In the following sections, we propose two methods. The first uses Python code with the Pandas library and traditional NLP techniques. The second prompts an LLM to explore and validate the data.

PYTHON CODE FOR EXPLORATION AND VALIDATION

As NLP has been used for data analysis for several decades, a vast collection of libraries is available for data exploration and validation. In this section, we present standard techniques for handling datasets, including tokenization and normalization. Tokenization is the process of breaking down a continuous text into smaller units called "tokens," which are often individual words or punctuation marks. Normalization involves transforming text into a consistent, standard format to reduce variations and simplify analysis. For example, the following code example uses "lowercase conversion" as a form of normalization, ensuring that "Hello," "hello," and "HELLO" are all treated as the same word. It can also

post_id		owner	post_date	post_text
0	1	Clean Lady	2023-11-01	🌎 As a climate activist, every day feels like a new opportunity to drive impactful change! 🔋 In …
1	2	Clean Lady	2023-11-02	Recycling isn't just about bins and labels—it's a way of life! ♻ In my recycling venture, I see…
2	3	Clean Lady	2023-11-03	🔧 Excited to announce that I'm collaborating with local businesses to implement a more robust re…
3	4	Clean Lady	2023-11-04	🌍 Did you know that recycling one aluminum can saves enough energy to power a TV for three hours…
4	5	Clean Lady	2023-11-05	As climate change accelerates, so does my passion for advocating for change! ⚡ Recently, I atte…

post_id		owner	post_date	post_text
1110	1111	Student-m	2023-11-25	In talking to fellow students, I recognize a shared passion for social equity through art. How d…
1111	1112	Student-m	2023-11-26	Events like idea labs and hackathons encourage interdisciplinary collaboration. I recently parti…
1112	1113	Student-m	2023-11-27	I've been reflecting on the role of education in shaping our worldviews. With so much informatio…
1113	1114	Student-m	2023-11-28	Art has a powerful ability to foster connections among diverse groups. I'm interested in creatin…
1114	1115	Student-m	2023-11-29	Closing out November with gratitude for the community I've found here. The discussions we have e…

Fig. 7.1 Dataframe of social media posts from the explore_dataframe.ipynb notebook

include removing punctuation and filtering out single-character terms. Lemmatization (not implemented in the sample code) is another normalization technique that reduces words to their base or dictionary form, known as a "lemma." For example, "running," "ran," and "runs" would all be lemmatized to "run," allowing for more accurate counting and analysis of the core meaning of words.

The following code counts the number of words, posts, and words per post for the fictional personas in the dataset and presents the results in a table format. The example code is contained in the data_exploration_standard.ipynb notebook, and an LLM-generated description of it can be found in the data_exploration_standard.html file.

The code examples presented throughout the book can be several pages long, making the navigation between the code and its explanation difficult. To make the navigation easier, the provided HTML files have a side-by-side layout that allows you to scroll through the code and its corresponding explanation independently. This helps read the text on the right pane while keeping the relevant code visible on the left pane, eliminating the need to flip back and forth between the code and the explanation.

Starting with this code example and throughout the rest of the book, each primary function includes a string (delimited by three quotation marks) that documents the objective of the function, the parameters needed, and the values returned. This is called a docstring, and it is the best practice in computer programming to include it in any sufficiently complex function.

```
1:     # Import libraries
2:     import pandas as pd
3:     import re
4:     from collections import Counter
5:     import nltk
6:     from nltk.corpus import stopwords
7:     from nltk.tokenize import RegexpTokenizer
8:     from IPython.display import display
9:
10:
11:     def process_text(df, text_column="post_text"):
12:         """Process text data in a DataFrame column using
           NLTK.
13:
```

(continued)

(continued)

```
14:              Uses NLTK for tokenization and text cleaning.
                 Handles normalization,
15:              removes stop words and punctuation, and returns
                 processed text as
16:              word lists.
17:              Includes lowercase conversion and filters
                 single-char terms.
18:
19:                :param df: Input DataFrame with text data
20:                :param text_column: Column name with text data
21:                :return: DataFrame with new 'processed_text'
                 column containing word
22:                lists
23:                """
24:              # Download required NLTK data if not already present
25:              try:
26:                  nltk.data.find("tokenizers/punkt")
27:                  nltk.data.find("corpora/stopwords")
28:              except LookupError:
29:                  nltk.download("punkt")
30:                  nltk.download("stopwords")
31:
32:              # Initialize tokenizer to remove punctuation
33:              tokenizer = RegexpTokenizer(r"\w+")
34:
35:              # Get English stop words
36:              stop_words = set(stopwords.words("english"))
37:
38:              # Process each text entry
39:              def process_single_text(text):
40:                  # Convert to lowercase and tokenize
41:                  words = tokenizer.tokenize(str(text).lower())
42:                  # Remove stop words and single characters
43:                  words = [w for w in words if w not in stop_words
                 and len(w) > 1]
44:                  return words
45:
46:              # Add processed text column
47:              df = df.copy()
48:              df["processed_text"] = df[text_
                 column].apply(process_single_text)
49:
50:              return df
51:
```

(continued)

(continued)

```
52:
53:        def get_word_frequencies(df, text_column="post_text",
           n_words=20):
54:            """Calculate word frequencies from a DataFrame's
           text column.
55:
56:            Uses processed text data to find the most frequent
           meaningful words.
57:            Relies on process_text function for preprocessing
           before counting
58:            frequencies.
59:
60:            :param df: Input DataFrame with text data
61:            :param text_column: Text column name, defaults to
           "post_text"
62:            :param n_words: Number of top words to return,
           defaults to 20
63:            :return: DataFrame with word counts, sorted by
           frequency
64:            """
65:            # Process text if not already processed
66:            if "processed_text" not in df.columns:
67:                df = process_text(df, text_column)
68:
69:            # Combine all processed words
70:            all_words = []
71:            for words in df["processed_text"]:
72:                all_words.extend(words)
73:
74:            # Count word frequencies
75:            word_freq = Counter(all_words)
76:
77:            # Convert to DataFrame
78:            df_frequencies = pd.DataFrame(
79:                word_freq.most_common(n_words),
           columns=["word", "count"]
80:            )
81:
82:            return df_frequencies
83:
84:
85:        def generate_metrics(df):
86:            """Generate text metrics for each individual in the
           DataFrame.
87:
```

(continued)

(continued)

88:	*Calculates metrics per individual using processed text data: word*
89:	*counts, post counts, and percentages across the dataset.*
90:	
91:	*:param df: DataFrame with 'owner' and 'processed_text' columns*
92:	*:return: DataFrame with metrics for each owner*
93:	*"""*
94:	*# Initialize metrics dictionary*
95:	metrics = {
96:	"count_posts": df.groupby("owner").size(),
97:	"count_words": df.groupby("owner")["processed_text"].apply(
98:	*# x: set of processed_text posts for each individual*
99:	*# words: list of words in each post*
100:	*# sum(): total word count across all posts per individual*
101:	**lambda** x: sum(len(words) **for** words **in** x)
102:	),
103:	"words_per_post": df.groupby("owner")["processed_text"].apply(
104:	*# x: set of owner's posts*
105:	**lambda** x: sum(len(words) **for** words **in** x)
106:	/ len(x)
107:	),
108:	}
109:	
110:	*# Count non-alphanumeric/whitespace chars (emojis)*
111:	**def** count_emojis(text):
112:	emoji_pattern = re.compile(r"[^\w\s]")
113:	**return** len(emoji_pattern.findall(text))
114:	
115:	metrics["count_emojis"] = df.groupby("owner")["post_text"].apply(
116:	**lambda** x: x.apply(count_emojis).sum()
117:	)
118:	
119:	*# Calculate percentages*
120:	total_words = metrics["count_words"].sum()
121:	total_posts = metrics["count_posts"].sum()
122:	
123:	metrics["pct_of_words"] = metrics["count_words"] / total_words * 100

(continued)

(continued)

```
124:            metrics["pct_of_posts"] = metrics["count_posts"] /
                total_posts * 100
125:
126:            # Combine all metrics into a DataFrame
127:            df_metrics = pd.DataFrame(metrics).round(3)
128:
129:            # Reorder columns for better readability
130:            column_order = [
131:                "count_emojis",
132:                "count_words",
133:                "count_posts",
134:                "words_per_post",
135:                "pct_of_words", # Percentage of words by owner
136:                "pct_of_posts", # Percentage of posts by owner
137:            ]
138:            df_metrics = df_metrics[column_order]
139:
140:            return df_metrics
141:
142:
143:        # Main execution
144:
145:        # Load social media posts from CSV file
146:        df_posts = pd.read_csv("../data/All_Synthetic_
                Data.csv")
147:
148:        # Process text and add processed_text column
149:        df_posts = process_text(df_posts)
150:
151:        # Perform word frequency analysis
152:        df_word_frequency = get_word_frequencies(df_posts)
153:
154:        # Generate text metrics for each owner
155:        df_metrics = generate_metrics(df_posts)
156:
157:        # Display results
158:        print("\nMost frequent words in social media posts:")
159:        display(df_word_frequency)
160:
161:        print("\nText metrics by owner:")
162:        display(df_metrics)
```

Lines 2 to 8 import the libraries and functions needed for data manipulation, text processing, and display results. Line 5 imports the Natural Language Toolkit (NLTK) library, which is used extensively in the script.

Lines 11 to 50 implement the `process_text()` function, which cleans and normalizes text in a designated column of a dataframe.

Lines 12 to 23 contain the docstring of the function. A docstring is a string literal used in Python to document a module, function, class, or method, providing a concise summary of its purpose and how to use it. The docstrings used in the code examples of this book follow the reStructuredText (reST) format. Another popular docstring format is the Google style.

Lines 25 to 30 load the required NLTK data.

Line 33 initializes a `RegexpTokenizer` with the pattern `r"\w+"`. This splits text into sequences of word characters (alphanumeric characters and underscores), removing punctuation and whitespace.

Line 36 retrieves the set of English stop words provided by the NLTK library and stores them in the `stop_words` variable. Using a set allows for very fast lookups.

Lines 39 to 44 define a nested helper function called `process_single_text()`, which takes as input a single string, converts it to lowercase, tokenizes it, and removes stop words.

Line 48 applies the `process_single_text()` function to each entry in the specified `text_column` of the dataframe. The results (lists of processed words) are stored in a new column of the dataframe named `"processed_text"`.

Line 50 returns the modified dataframe with the new `"processed_text"` column.

Lines 53 to 82 define the `get_word_frequency()` function that computes the most frequent words. The function takes as input a dataframe, an optional `text_column` parameter that defaults to `"post_text"`, and an optional `n_words` parameter indicating the number of top words to return, which defaults to 20.

Lines 66 and 67 check if a `"processed_text"` column already exists in the dataframe. If not, the `process_text()` function is called to preprocess the text and add it to that column.

Line 70 initializes an empty list called `all_words`. Lines 71 to 72 iterate through the `"processed_text"` column, which contains lists of words, and extend the `all_words` list with all individual words from these lists. This effectively flattens the list of lists into a single list of all words.

Line 75 uses `Counter(all_words)` to create a dictionary-like object where keys are words and values are their frequencies.

Lines 78 to 80 convert the word frequencies into a Pandas dataframe. The `word_freq.most_common(n_words)` method returns a list of the `n_words` most common words and their counts as tuples, which are then used to create a dataframe with columns "word" and "count". A tuple in Python is an ordered collection of items enclosed in parenthesis. A tuple is different from a list in that it is immutable, i.e., once it is created, it cannot be modified.

Line 82 returns the dataframe containing the top word frequencies.

Lines 85 to 140 define the `generate_metrics()` function that computes various text-related metrics for each fictional owner in the dataframe. The function takes a dataframe as input.

Lines 95 to 107 initialize a Python dictionary called `metrics` that define each "owner" "count_posts," "count_words," and "words_per_post" value. The latter is the average number of words per post.

Lines 111 to 113 define a nested helper function called `count_emojis` that takes a string and uses a regular expression `r"[^\w\s]"` to match any character that is NOT a word character (alphanumeric + underscore) and NOT a whitespace character. A regular expression (regex) is a sequence of characters that defines a search pattern, which is primarily used for matching, locating, and manipulating strings of text.

Lines 115 to 117 calculate the total count of "emojis" (as defined by the regex pattern) for each fictional owner.

Lines 120 to 121 calculate the total number of words and posts across the entire dataset from the previously computed metrics.

Lines 123 to 124 calculate the fraction of total words and posts contributed by each fictional owner by dividing their respective counts by the dataset totals and multiplying by 100. These percentages are added to the metrics dictionary.

Line 127 converts the metric dictionary into a Pandas dataframe and rounds all the numerical values to 3 decimal places.

Lines 130 to 136 define a specific order for the columns in the dataframe for better readability. Line 138 reorders the columns of the `df_metrics` dataframe according to the defined `column_order`.

Line 140 returns the dataframe containing the generated metrics per owner.

Lines 146 to 162 organize the execution of the functions to perform the analysis and display the results. Line 146 loads the "All_Synthetic_Data.csv" file into a dataframe called df_posts. Line 149 calls the process_text() function on the df_posts dataframe, which adds the "processed_text" column to the dataframe, containing cleaned and tokenized words for each post. Line 152 calls the get_word_frequencies() function on the df_posts dataframe. This computes the most frequent words and their counts, storing the result in a dataframe called df_word_frequency. Line 155 calls the generate_metrics() function on the df_posts dataframe. The result is stored in a dataframe called df_metrics. Finally, lines 158 to 162 print descriptive headers and display the content of the df_word_frequency and df_metrics dataframes.

Figure 7.2 shows the output of the above code. Note in the first table that the row count starts at zero and not one.

DATA EXPLORATION AND VALIDATION VIA LLM-BASED APPROACHES

In this subsection, we explore two LLM-based approaches to count the most frequent words. In the first approach, we create a prompt containing all the posts in the dataset and instruct the model in natural language to (a) preprocess the posts and (b) return the list of the 20 most frequent words. In the second approach, we create a prompt with instructions to write a Python function that preprocesses the posts and then returns the list of the 20 most frequent words. The difference is that in the first case, we ask the LLM to directly produce the word frequency table, whereas in the second case, we ask the LLM to *write a program* that produces the table. The latter is a simple example of how coders use LLMs to write software.

The following is the code for the first approach using the OpenAI GPT o4-mini model. The code is also available in the data_exploration_gpt.ipynb notebook. As several Python programming concepts have already been introduced in the previous code examples, for brevity, in this code example, we explain only the new concepts. However, a detailed LLM-generated description of the entire code is still available in the data_exploration_gpt.html file.

Most frequent words in social media posts:

	word	count
0	let	341
1	health	302
2	art	180
3	fintech	173
4	women	161
5	healthcare	134
6	must	132
7	community	130
8	financial	130
9	change	128
10	innovation	127
11	students	124
12	work	122
13	family	115
14	technology	114
15	future	108
16	importance	107
17	energy	106
18	today	106
19	new	105

Text metrics by owner:

owner	count_emojis	count_words	count_posts	words_per_post	pct_of_words	pct_of_posts
Clean Lady	1236	3022	100	30.220	10.618	8.969
Lady FinTech	1018	3324	130	25.569	11.679	11.659
Lady equality	1025	3052	110	27.745	10.723	9.865
Medical-f	798	3002	140	21.443	10.548	12.556
Medical-m	702	2756	110	25.055	9.683	9.865
Mr Equality	349	1368	40	34.200	4.807	3.587
Mr FinTech	894	3618	125	28.944	12.712	11.211
Mr energy	831	3325	140	23.750	11.683	12.556
Student-f	783	2681	110	24.373	9.420	9.865
Student-m	589	2313	110	21.027	8.127	9.865

Fig. 7.2 Data exploration output from the data_exploration_standard.ipynb notebook

```
1:              # Import libraries
2:              import os
3:              import json
4:              import pandas as pd
5:              from openai import OpenAI
6:              from dotenv import load_dotenv
7:              from nltk.corpus import stopwords
8:              from IPython.display import display
9:
10:             # Load environment variables from .env file
11:             load_dotenv()
12:
13:             # Define constants
14:             delimiter = "###"
15:
16:
17:             def generate_prompt(posts):
18:                 """Generate a prompt for analyzing word
                    frequencies.
19:
20:                     This function creates a prompt to find
                    frequent words
21:                     in social media posts. It specifies the
                    response format
22:                     and excludes stop words.
23:
24:                         :param posts: Post texts concatenated with
                    delimiters
25:                         :return: List of messages for OpenAI API
                    with prompts
26:                     """
27:
28:                     # Get English stop words
29:                     stop_words =
                    set(stopwords.words("english"))
30:
31:                     system_message = """
32:                         You're a helpful assistant.
33:                         Your task is to analyze social media
                    posts.
34:                     """
35:                     user_message = f"""
36:                         Below are social media posts delimited
                    with {delimiter}.
```

(continued)

(continued)

```
37:                    Find the 20 most frequent words and
           count their occurrences.
38:                    As pre-processing convert text to lower
           case, tokenize words
39:                    and exclude the following stop words:
           {stop_words}.
40:                    Return results in descending order of
           frequency.
41:                    Use this JSON format:
42:
43:                    "results": [
44:                        {{"word": "support", "count": 4}},
45:                        {{"word": "community", "count":
           3}},
46:                        ...
47:                    ]
48:
49:                    Social media posts: {posts}
50:                """
51:            messages = [
52:                {"role": "system", "content": system_
           message},
53:                {"role": "user", "content": user_
           message},
54:            ]
55:
56:            return messages
57:
58:
59:        def get_model_response(messages, client,
           model="gpt-o4-mini"):
60:            """Send messages to API and get the response
           in JSON format.
61:
62:            This function sends a prompt to the API and
           gets a JSON response.
63:            It configures the API call to request JSON
           output format.
64:
65:            :param messages: Message dictionaries for
           OpenAI Chat API
66:            :param client: OpenAI client instance
67:            :param model: Model name, defaults to
           "gpt-4o-mini"
68:            :return: JSON-formatted response string
```

(continued)

(continued)

69:	"""
70:	
71:	result = client.chat.completions.create(
72:	model=model, messages=messages, response_format={
73:	"type": "json_object"
74:	}
75:	)
76:	
77:	**return** result.choices[0].message.content
78:	
79:	
80:	# *Retrieve OpenAI API key from environment variable*
81:	api_key = os.getenv("OPENAI_API_KEY")
82:	**if not** api_key:
83:	**raise ValueError**("Missing OPENAI_API_KEY in environment or .env file")
84:	
85:	# *Initialize OpenAI client*
86:	client = OpenAI(api_key=api_key)
87:	
88:	# *Load social media posts from CSV file*
89:	df_posts = pd.read_csv("../data/All_Synthetic_Data.csv")
90:	
91:	# *Prepare string of posts with delimiters*
92:	posts_string = delimiter.join(df_posts.post_text.values)
93:	
94:	# *Generate and send prompt to GPT model*
95:	prompt = generate_prompt(posts_string)
96:	result = get_model_response(prompt, client)
97:	
98:	# *Convert JSON string to Python dictionary*
99:	json_data = json.loads(result)
100:	
101:	# *Create DataFrame from results and sort by count*
102:	df_word_counts = (
103:	pd.DataFrame(json_data["results"])
104:	.sort_values("count", ascending=**False**)
105:	.reset_index(drop=**True**)
106:	)
107:	

(continued)

(continued)

108:	`# Display results`
109:	`print("Most frequent words in social media posts:")`
110:	`display(df_word_counts)`

Lines 2 to 8 import the required libraries and functions. Line 3 imports the `json` library. JSON (JavaScript Object Notation) is a text-based data-interchange format that is easy for humans to read and write and easy for machines to generate and parse. Since LLMs produce primarily text, the data format is used to convert JSON-formatted strings generated by LLMs into Python data structures such as lists and dictionaries. This format facilitates data processing and analysis.

Line 14 defines a string constant `"###"` named `delimiter` used to separate individual social media posts passed in the prompt to the LLM.

Lines 17 to 56 define a function named `generate_prompt()` that takes as input a string containing the complete set of social media posts, delimited by the `"###"` string, and returns the list of system and user messages for the OpenAI API. Line 29 retrieves the standard list of English stop words from the NLTK library, as in the previous code example. These words will be provided in the prompt to the LLM to be excluded from frequency counts. Lines 35 to 47 define the user message with instructions about the preprocessing steps and what needs to be returned. The instructions define a specific JSON format for the output, including an example, to ensure that the response can be easily converted into a Python data structure (lines 41 to 47). Lines 51 to 54 create the list of system and user messages, and line 56 returns the list.

Lines 59 to 77 define a `get_model_response()` function that takes three arguments: a list of messages for the API, an initialized OpenAI API client, and the name of the model to be used. Lines 71 to 75 make the call to the API. The `response_format` parameter indicates that the response must be in JSON format. Line 77 extracts the text content from the result object returned by the API.

Lines 80 to 106 represent the main execution block that organizes the execution of the different steps.

Line 86 initializes an OpenAI API client, and line 89 loads the content of the `"All_Synthetic_Data.csv"` file into a dataframe named `df_posts`.

Line 92 retrieves the list of strings in the "post_text" column of the dataframe (the social media posts) and combines them into a single string of posts separated by the "###" delimiter. For example, if the "post_text" column of the dataframe contains two posts, such as "This is a first post" and "The car is red", the value stored in the posts_string variable is "This is a first post###The car is red".

Line 95 generates the messages for the OpenAI API, and line 96 sends the messages to the model through the get_model_response() function, storing the response text in the result variable.

Line 99 parses the result string (which is in JSON format) into a Python dictionary named json_data.

Lines 102 to 106 create a dataframe named df_word_counts with columns "word" and "count" and sort the entries in descending order of the count value.

Finally, line 110 displays the df_word_counts dataframe.

The previous code was run three times. The results of each execution are shown in Fig. 7.3. Note that the results are different, not only from one execution to another but also with respect to the results produced by the data_exploration_standard.ipynb notebook and shown in Fig. 7.2. We use the results from that notebook as a validation reference, or ground truth, since we were able to validate the step-by-step process to produce those numbers.

The inaccuracy of the LLM results with respect to the ground truth indicates that this is not a reliable method for the task. This example highlights a critical limitation of LLMs: despite their capacity for producing plausible language, they lack the ability to produce accurate numerical results. Therefore, tasks requiring accurate numerical results need alternative approaches. We present a second approach in which an LLM is used as a coding assistant. We present the first approach, despite the inaccuracy of the results, to provide a concrete example of LLM limitations and to emphasize the need for researchers to review LLM output critically.

In the second approach, we create a prompt with instructions to write a Python function that preprocesses the posts and then returns the list of the 20 most frequent words. The following prompt was sent to the Gemini API via the gemini-2.5-pro model:

```
f"""
    Given a pandas dataframe containing a column called "post_
text"
```

	word	count		word	count		word	count
0	recycling	40	0	recycling	75	0	community	40
1	community	25	1	community	60	1	recycling	30
2	sustainability	23	2	sustainability	55	2	technology	23
3	climate	22	3	climate	50	3	finance	20
4	waste	20	4	change	48	4	financial	20
5	impact	18	5	technology	45	5	art	20
6	students	18	6	innovation	42	6	sustainability	20
7	education	17	7	environment	40	7	innovation	15
8	action	17	8	education	38	8	social	15
9	economy	16	9	students	36	9	change	15
10	circular	16	10	business	35	10	education	11
11	planet	14	11	data	34	11	students	10
12	innovation	13	12	health	33	12	data	10
13	technology	13	13	project	31	13	policy	10
14	energy	12	14	local	30	14	business	10
15	business	12	15	economy	29	15	climate	10
16	change	12	16	policy	28	16	energy	9
17	art	11	17	art	27	17	economy	8
18	future	11	18	digital	26	18	global	5
19	family	10	19	social	25	19	diversity	5

Fig. 7.3   LLM's data exploration output from the data_exploration_gpt.ipynb notebook

type: string), write a function that takes as input that dataframe
and returns a dataframe with two columns: "word" and "count". The
output dataframe contains in descending order, the N = 20 most frequent
words in the "post_text" column of the input dataframe. The entries
in the "post_text" column must be preprocessed: convert strings to

```
    lower case, tokenize words, remove English stop words, and
remove
    single-character words.
" " "
```

When working with LLMs as coding assistants, as in this case, readers need to assume that the generated code is not directly usable and requires review and adjustment. The result from the prompt above was slightly edited to replace a word_tokenize function, which caused an execution error, with a RegexpTokenizer function. The modified code was stored in the data_exploration_gemini_output_ code.py script. The references to the replaced word_tokenize function were left as comments for the reader to understand what was changed. An LLM-generated description of the code is available in the data_exploration_gemini_output_code.html file. For brevity, we do not provide a step-by-step description of that script since it is essentially the same logic implemented in the process_text() and get_word_frequencies() functions of the data_exploration_ standard.ipynb notebook, but in a single function get_top_n_ words().

The word frequency analysis example demonstrates several key points about LLMs. First, users must critically evaluate their output both qualitatively and quantitatively. Ground truth data are needed for quantitative validation. Second, for tasks requiring numerical accuracy, alternative solutions such as code generation should be considered. Third, any code generated by an LLM must also be carefully reviewed for errors to ensure that it performs the intended task. As LLMs continue to evolve, it remains crucial for researchers to understand their capabilities and limitations.

CHAPTER 8

Classification

Abstract This chapter provides an overview of classification, a key method in data analysis. It explains different techniques for data classification using large language models (LLMs), including open-access models and detailed prompts for zero-shot, one-shot, and few-shot classifications. The chapter illustrates how LLMs can enhance qualitative analysis by leveraging their classification capabilities. Additionally, the chapter discusses the importance of prompt design and the cautious use of LLMs. This suggests techniques for improving reliability and the use of balanced approaches when selecting methods for specific research objectives.

Keywords Shot-classification · Sentiment analysis · Large language models

Classification is a technique widely used in data analysis to organize data points into predefined groups or classes on the basis of their characteristics. There are three types of classification: binary, multiclass, and multilabel. Binary classification involves predicting one of two possible classes, such as "yes" vs "no" or "disease" vs "no disease." Multiclass classification involves predicting one of more than two possible classes, for example, classifying images of animals into "dog," "cat," "monkey," etc. In multilabel classification, a single data point may belong

© The Author(s) 2026
D. Garcia Quevedo and J. Kuri, *AI for Qualitative Research*,
https://doi.org/10.1007/978-3-032-08872-7_8

to multiple classes simultaneously. For example, an image can be classified as "mountain," "lake," and "sunset."

Classification techniques have significantly evolved over time. Historically, supervised machine learning approaches have been used, where a model is first trained on labeled data. An example of a labeled dataset is a collection of emails, each labeled as either "spam" or "no spam." After training, the model is used to predict the class(es) to which new, unlabeled data points belong. A key limitation of this approach is the reliance on labeled data. Labeling is usually a manual process, which restricts the amount of training data available. Despite this limitation, classification is widely used in applications such as spam detection, image recognition, medical diagnosis, credit scoring, and fraud detection.

Classification algorithms are crucial tools for data analysis and play an important role in extracting meaningful insights from complex datasets. A common application of classification in management research is sentiment analysis, which consists of classifying the sentiment of expressions as positive, negative, or neutral. Researchers have long used sentiment analysis to analyze emotional expressions in documents, customer feedback and reviews, social media posts, and blogs. Other forms of classification include the identification of emotions such as sadness, anger, or happiness, as well as the identification of stance ("approval" vs "rejection") in the analysis of political discourse.

Qualitative analysis is a form of classification in which data are grouped into categories that convey the same idea, meaning, or explanation (Charmaz & Thornberg, 2021; Grodal et al., 2021; Saldaña, 2013). The traditional approach of supervised learning on labeled data for narrowly defined tasks is rigid; therefore, qualitative researchers are skeptical of using these tools to support their analysis. LLMs help address this limitation since they can be used as general-purpose classifiers that rely on their statistical representation of language rather than on training on labeled data. Researchers can leverage this flexibility to automatically categorize large datasets through prompt engineering and streamline their analysis process.

Understanding Classification with LLMs

Owing to their ability to capture and process the context and semantics of text data, LLMs have created new avenues for qualitative analysis. Unlike previous classifiers that relied on labeled data, LLMs can classify data via simple instructions, known as prompts. They leverage their statistical representation of language to classify data in both structured formats, such as text records in databases, and unstructured formats, such as free-form text in documents. In addition, their ability to generalize across domains and learn new information from the user's prompt makes them very versatile and adaptable to a variety of research projects. In particular, LLMs' capabilities to adapt to domain-specific situations via in-context learning, where a model learns to perform a new task using the information provided directly within the prompt, offer the flexibility needed for qualitative analysis. As such, LLMs' extended capabilities are particularly interesting for qualitative researchers, who focus primarily on unstructured data such as interviews, archival documents, and observations. These capabilities can be leveraged through prompt techniques such as zero-shot, one-shot, and few-shot classifications.

Zero-shot classification is the simplest way of instructing an LLM to perform a classification. In this approach, the user provides the LLM with explicit instructions on how to classify the input data but without providing any examples. The model relies entirely on its pretrained understanding of the given instructions to execute the classification. This form of classification requires minimal prompt elaboration but can be less accurate than other approaches, as the model receives limited guidance. For example, the following prompt can be used to perform a sentiment analysis task:

```
Prompt: f"""Classify the following review as expressing a
positive, negative,
or neutral sentiment: {input_text}. There can only be one class.
"""
```

In one-shot classification, the model is given instructions and an input–output example to describe the task further. This additional context is used to improve performance relative to zero-shot classification for the intended task. The example helps clarify the instructions, but the model still relies primarily on its pretrained understanding. Using the previous example for sentiment analysis, a one-shot classification prompt would be as follows:

```
Prompt: f"""Classify the following review as expressing a
positive, negative,
or neutral sentiment: {input_text}. There can only be one class.
Example:
The service was excellent. Output: Positive."""
```

Few-shot classification provides the model with a small number of input–output examples, adding more context to the instructions. These examples help the model understand the specific format, nuances, or desired categories for the classification task. This approach is often more effective than previous approaches, especially for domain-specific or ambiguous classifications. It is recommended for complex or domain-specific tasks when labeled examples are available. In the following example, the LLM observes the pattern of review-to-sentiment mappings from the three examples. It learns the expected output format and the specific criteria for each sentiment category, as demonstrated by the examples:

```
Prompt: f"""Classify the following review as expressing a
positive, negative,
or neutral sentiment: {input_text}. There can only be one class.
Examples:
1) The service was excellent. Output: Positive;
2) The food was bad. Output: Negative;
3) The experience was OK. Output: Neutral."""
```

In summary, classification leveraging in-context learning offers (1) flexibility; (2) reduces the need for labeled data since only a few labeled examples are needed; (3) facilitates quick experimentation with different classifications; and (4) enables domain adaptation, allowing the classification logic to be tuned to the nuances of a specific field. However, there are potential limitations. First, the classification can be highly sensitive to the exact wording and order of examples in the prompt. Second, the number of examples that can be provided is limited by the model's context size.

Third, the model's performance may not be as accurate as the performance of a fine-tuned model. To mitigate these limitations, researchers could turn to fine-tuning.

Fine-tuning refers to further training an LLM using a specialized dataset tailored to a specific task or domain and training procedures such as reinforcement learning with human feedback (RLHF) (Ouyang et al., 2022). This process adjusts the model's parameters to the specialized task, thereby improving performance. It aims at outputs that are more accurate and relevant to the specific requirements of the target application. Although fine-tuning may not require a labeled dataset as large as for supervised learning, the model still needs a labeled dataset for training. Moreover, programming skills are required to perform fine-tuning. Fortunately, for common NLP tasks such as sentiment analysis, fine-tuned LLMs are available in popular hosting platforms such as HuggingFace.

Many early fine-tuned LLMs were based on open-source models that provide a detailed explanation of their training data and fine-tuning procedure. This presents a significant advantage for researchers, as the training parameters and objectives are clearly stated, allowing for better understanding and control of the outputs. Proprietary models, on the other hand, generally have better performance than open models do and allow for adaptability through prompt engineering. However, the lack of detail on their training data and procedures prevents researchers from fully understanding their output.

In the following section, we provide examples of how to apply the prompting techniques mentioned above. Although fine-tuning requires coding skills, numerous fine-tuned models are available, making them accessible and easy to use for researchers with limited coding experience. The following section explains how to utilize an open-source fine-tuned model and how to adapt a theoretical framework to perform zero-shot, one-shot, and few-shot classification.

CREATING A CLASSIFICATION FOR A RESEARCH PROJECT

In this section, we provide examples of how to use LLMs for classification using the synthetic data provided with the book. Through the GitHub repository provided with the book, these examples can be downloaded to start a first analysis. To explain in-context learning classification, we draw on the theoretical context presented in Garcia Quevedo et al. (2025) to illustrate how these types of prompts can be adapted to address specific research questions.

Fine-Tuned LLMs for Common Classifications

As many open-source fine-tuned models are published with an explanation of the data and procedures used for training, we favor these models. The transparency of these models helps to increase confidence, as the performance of LLMs is tied to domain-specific labeled data. We recommend that, when available, researchers carefully review this information to determine if a particular model is suitable for a specific research project. Next, we provide the code and explanation of two fine-tuned LLMs for classification purposes.

Example 1—Sentiment Analysis
The model used in this example is part of the TweetNLP library developed by Camacho-Collados and colleagues (2022) for analysis of Twitter and social media data. The library is accessible through GitHub (https://github.com/cardiffnlp/tweetnlp) and the HuggingFace platform (https://huggingface.co/collections/cardiffnlp/tweetnlp). The library leverages LLMs tuned for social media and provides functions for sentiment analysis, emoji prediction, emotion detection, etc. (Camacho-collados et al., 2022). From the TweetNLP library, we selected the multilingual model developed by Barbieri et al. (2022). In their paper, the authors explained the training parameters and the evaluation criteria used to fine-tune the model for sentiment analysis of social media posts (Barbieri et al., 2022). As many common NLP tasks have been standardized, open-source, ready-to-use models are a great starting point for research projects since they save time and effort. However, researchers need to understand model details to determine if they are suitable for their needs. For example, a model trained on tweets may not be suitable for other forms of text, such as interviews or content from a specialized domain.

The following code classifies social media posts into positive, negative, or neutral. The code is also available in the `sentiment_analysis_hf.ipynb` notebook. This script uses the same code structure for image classification presented in Chapter 5. For brevity, we explain only the new lines of code and skip the details already explained in the previous sections. The detailed LLM-generated description of the code is available in the `sentiment_analysis_hf.html` file.

```
1:    import pandas as pd
2:    from transformers import pipeline
3:    from IPython.display import display
4:
5:    # Load the synthetic social media data
6:    df_posts = pd.read_csv("../data/All_Synthetic_
      Data.csv")
7:
8:    # Create a sentiment analysis task using Hugging
      Face Transformers
9:    sentiment_task = pipeline(
10:       "sentiment-analysis",
11:       model="cardiffnlp/
      twitter-xlm-roberta-base-sentiment",
12:   )
13:
14:   # Store the posts into a list
15:   docs = df_posts.post_text.tolist()
16:
17:   # Perform sentiment analysis on each post. Store
      results in DataFrame
18:   for doc in docs:
19:       result = sentiment_task(doc)
20:       label = result[0]["label"]
21:       score = result[0]["score"]
22:       df_posts.loc[df_posts["post_text"] == doc,
      "sentiment"] = label
23:       df_posts.loc[df_posts["post_text"] == doc,
      "score"] = score
24:
25:   # Display the DataFrame with sentiment analysis
      results
26:   display(df_posts)
```

Lines 1 to 12 import the necessary libraries, load the dataset, and create a sentiment analysis task via the `cardiffnlp/twitter-xlm-roberta-base-sentiment` model. These steps have been explained in detail in Chapter 5, although in this case, we create a sentiment analysis task instead of a translation or image classification task.

Through lines 15 to 23, we explain how to transform the posts into a list and how to create a loop to assign a classification label and a score to each post.

Line 15 extracts the text content from the `'post_text'` column of the `df_posts` dataframe and converts it into a Python list. This list, named `docs`, contains each individual social media post as a string that is ready to be processed by the sentiment analysis task.

Lines 18 to 23 iterate through the list to execute the sentiment analysis task and store the results. Line 18 starts a `for` loop that iterates over each string in the `docs` list. Line 19 passes the current post text (in the doc variable) to the initialized `sentiment_task` pipeline. The pipeline processes the text and returns a list containing a Python dictionary with the sentiment analysis result. The dictionary contains a `"label"` and a `"score"` entry. Lines 20 and 21 extract the values of these entries from the dictionary. Lines 22 and 23 use the Pandas' `loc` function to locate the row in the `df_posts` dataframe that corresponds to the current value of the `doc` variable (by matching it with the value in the `'post_text'` column) and then assign the extracted label and score values to new columns named `'sentiment'` and `'score'` for that row.

Line 26 displays the entire `df_posts` dataframe, which contains the original social media posts along with the newly added `'sentiment'` and `'score'` columns. The output is shown in Fig. 8.1.

Example 2—Emotion classification
The following example uses an open-source LLM developed by an AI research team at Meta (https://huggingface.co/facebook/bart-large-mnli). The model was pretrained for natural language generation, translation, and comprehension (Lewis et al., 2019). This base model was then adapted for zero-shot classification via the method described by Yin et al. (2019). This algorithm performs well with specific, concrete categories, such as sentiment, emotion, or activity classification, offering a flexible way to customize classifiers. However, its classification ability is tied to its training data, which constitute the generic multi-genre natural language inference (MNLI) corpus. This model is also simple for noncoders to use. Below, we demonstrate how to classify social media posts as expressing anticipation, joy, trust, fear, surprise, sadness, disgust, and anger.

This code is found under the name `zero_shot_classification_hf.ipynb`, and the LLM-generated description is under the `zero_shot_classification_hf.html` file. This code also uses a loop to

post_id	owner	post_date	post_text	sentiment	score
0	1	Clean Lady	2023-11-01	🌑 As a climate activist, every day feels like …	positive	0.508234
1	2	Clean Lady	2023-11-02	Recycling isn't just about bins and labels—it'…	neutral	0.438066
2	3	Clean Lady	2023-11-03	☞ Excited to announce that I'm collaborating w…	positive	0.769481
3	4	Clean Lady	2023-11-04	🌑 Did you know that recycling one aluminum can…	neutral	0.404816
4	5	Clean Lady	2023-11-05	As climate change accelerates, so does my pass…	positive	0.708418
…	…	…	…	…	…	…
1110	1111	Student-m	2023-11-25	In talking to fellow students, I recognize a s…	positive	0.689349
1111	1112	Student-m	2023-11-26	Events like idea labs and hackathons encourage…	positive	0.772510
1112	1113	Student-m	2023-11-27	I've been reflecting on the role of education …	positive	0.679100
1113	1114	Student-m	2023-11-28	Art has a powerful ability to foster connectio…	positive	0.756369
1114	1115	Student-m	2023-11-29	Closing out November with gratitude for the co…	positive	0.933021

Fig. 8.1 Sentiment analysis output from the sentiment_analysis_hf.ipynb notebook

assign labels to each post. In the previous example, only one label is assigned to each post; in this case, multiple labels are assigned. The results display each post with all the labels and their corresponding scores.

```
1:     import pandas as pd
2:     from transformers import pipeline
3:
4:     # Load the synthetic social media data
5:     df_posts = pd.read_csv("../data/All_Synthetic_Data.csv")
6:
7:     # Create a zero-shot classification task using Hugging Face
       Transformers
8:     zero_shot_task = pipeline(
9:         "zero-shot-classification",
10:        model="facebook/bart-large-mnli",
11:    )
12:
13:    # Define the candidate labels
14:    candidate_labels = [
15:        "Anticipation",
16:        "Joy",
17:        "Trust",
18:        "Fear",
19:        "Surprise",
20:        "Sadness",
21:        "Disgust",
22:        "Anger",
23:    ]
24:
25:    # Store the posts into a list
26:    docs = df_posts.post_text.tolist()
27:
28:    # For each post, perform classifiction and print result
29:    fordoc indocs:
30:        result = zero_shot_task(doc, candidate_labels)
31:        print(f"Post: {doc}")
32:        forlabel, score inzip(result["labels"],
       result["scores"]):
33:            print(f" - {label}: \t{score:.2f}")
```

Lines 1 to 11 import the libraries, load the dataset, and initialize a zero-shot classification pipeline using the "facebook/bart-large-mnli" model.

Lines 14 to 23 create a Python list named `candidate_labels` containing various emotion words. These labels represent the possible categories into which the zero-shot model will classify each social media post.

Line 26 extracts the text content from the `'post_text'` column of the `df_posts` dataframe and converts it into a Python list.

Lines 29 to 33 iterate through the posts, classify them, and display the results. Line 29 starts a `for` loop that iterates over each string in the `docs` list. Line 30 passes the current post text (in the `doc` variable) and the list of candidate labels to the initialized `zero_shot_task` pipeline. Line 31 prints the content of the current post, and lines 32 to 33 print each candidate label for that post along with its associated confidence score formatted to two decimal places. The `\t` creates a tab space for better alignment in the output, which provides a clear breakdown of the model's prediction for each emotion. Figure 8.2 shows the labels and scores for one post.

Post: 🌍 As a climate activist, every day feels like a new opportunity to drive impactful change! 🌱 In my experience working with universities, I'm often surprised by the lack of engagement in sustainability practices among students. As a solution, I propose integrating waste management and recycling into the curriculum. Imagine the impact we could have if every student graduated with a solid understanding of how to minimize waste and promote a circular economy! 💚 Let's empower the next generation to make sustainable choices. Who's with me? #Sustainability #Education #CircularEconomy

- Surprise: 0.66

- Anticipation: 0.11

- Joy: 0.11

- Trust: 0.06

- Fear: 0.02

- Anger: 0.01

- Disgust: 0.01

- Sadness: 0.01

Fig. 8.2 Emotion classification output from the zero_shot_classification_hf.ipynb notebook

While these models may excel at specific tasks, they require careful consideration of their training objectives since they determine their performance. An algorithm optimized for one objective may not align with the requirements of a specific research question. In the following section, we explore how to adapt a theoretical framework from a specific project to create a targeted classification that better suits the needs of a research project.

Zero-Shot, One-Shot, and Few-Shot Classifications

Proprietary models offer the advantages of great adaptability and customization, allowing the incorporation of theoretical frameworks to obtain a targeted classification. Thus, they can be customized to a greater extent, fitting many research projects. However, the use of these models has important limitations. As explained in Chapter 2, users have limited knowledge of the training data and parameters of these models, which makes them somewhat obscure and limits the ability to explain their outputs. Furthermore, the free service of most proprietary models will retain the processed data for training purposes. This may lead to data protection issues when sensitive or proprietary information is analyzed. We thus recommend using their paid service. The cost depends on the size of the data and the type of model employed to process it. Researchers should balance these limitations against their versatility, accessibility, flexibility, and performance.

Zero-shot, one-shot, and few-shot classifications require a well-elaborated prompt containing precise and complete information. As such, shot classification for research purposes requires deep knowledge of the literature. The construction of prompts for domain-specific classification and their output relies on the mastery of the theoretical framework. Therefore, we first need to review the theoretical framework used to illustrate shot classification.

We follow the theoretical context used by Garcia Quevedo et al. (2025) to demonstrate their method. In their paper, the authors mobilized the theory of impression management (IM) developed by Jones and Pittman (1982) in the context of the self-promotion of ecological ventures online. Jones and Pittman proposed five behaviors of assertive impression management: ingratiation to be liked, self-promotion to look competent, exemplification to show dedication, intimidation to seem powerful, and supplication to appear needy (Jones & Pittman, 1982). To demonstrate their method, Garcia Quevedo and colleagues investigated the types of IM behaviors used by men and women entrepreneurs on social media and how these tactics are gendered. As such, they limited the analysis to three behaviors: self-promotion, supplication, and ingratiation.

Once the theoretical framework is established and the classification objective is clear, we can start crafting the prompt. In their article, the authors aimed to identify posts that express IM behaviors by first examining the sentiment of the posts. The authors identified posts that expressed self-promotion, ingratiation, or supplication via sentiment analysis, selecting those classified as positive, negative, or neutral with the highest scores. Then, they read these posts to determine if they expressed IM behaviors. By doing so, the authors read many posts unrelated to IM behaviors, as sentiment analysis can provide only the emotional tone of each post. In this section, we leverage the versatility of LLMs to develop a target classification that aligns with the research questions. The examples presented below are crafted to identify the posts expressing self-promotion, ingratiation, and supplication.

The following is a code example of zero-shot classification using the OpenAI gpt-4o-mini model and a prompt based on the IM literature for target classification. The code is available in the zero_shot_classification_IM_gpt.ipynb notebook. An LLM-generated description of the code is available in the zero_shot_classification_IM_gpt.html file. The code is presented in four parts: generate the prompt, send the prompt to the LLM, generate the classification for each post, and finally display and save the results to a file. For brevity, we skip some of the details already explained for the previous scripts.

```
1:    # Import libraries
2:    import os
3:    import pandas as pd
4:    from openai import OpenAI
5:    from dotenv import load_dotenv
6:    from IPython.display import display
7:
8:    # File paths
9:    csv_path = "../data/All_Synthetic_Data.csv"
10:   parquet_path = "../data/All_Synthetic_Data_with_zero_
      shot.parquet"
11:
12:   def generate_classification_prompt(doc):
```

(continued)

(continued)

```
13:            """Generate a prompt for classifying social media
               posts.
14:
15:            Creates a prompt for OpenAI API to classify posts into
               impression
16:            management categories: self-promotion, ingratiation,
               or supplication.
17:            Uses delimiters for content separation.
18:
19:            :param doc: The social media post text to be
               classified
20:            :return: List of messages for OpenAI API with system
               and user prompts
21:            """
22:
23:            delimiter = "###"
24:            system_message = """
25:                You're a helpful assistant.
26:                Your task is to analyze social media posts.
27:            """
28:            user_message = f"""
29:                Below is a social media post delimited with
               {delimiter}.
30:                Identify the main category of this post as either
31:                self-promotion, ingratiation, or supplication.
32:                Output only the word "self-promotion",
               "ingratiation" or
33:                "supplication".
34:                If post is none of these, return the word "None".
35:
36:                Social media post: {delimiter}{doc}{delimiter}
37:            """
38:            messages = [
39:                {"role": "system", "content": system_message},
40:                {"role": "user", "content": user_message},
41:            ]
42:            return messages
43:
44:
45:    defget_model_response(messages, client,
           model="gpt-4o-mini"):
46:            """Send messages to OpenAI API and get response.
47:
48:            Sends a formatted prompt to OpenAI API and returns
               response text.
```

(continued)

(continued)

```
49:
50:              :param messages: List of message dictionaries for
            OpenAI Chat API
51:              :param client: OpenAI client instance for API calls
52:              :param model: OpenAI model name, defaults to
            "gpt-4o-mini"
53:              :return: Model's response text
54:              """
55:
56:              result = client.chat.completions.create(
57:                  model=model,
58:                  messages=messages
59:              )
60:              return result.choices[0].message.content
61:
62:
63:      def assign_classification(df_posts, client):
64:              """Classify social media posts using OpenAI API.
65:
66:              Process posts, generate prompts, get model responses,
            assign
67:              classifications categories: 'self-promotion',
            'ingratiation',
68:              'supplication', or 'None'.
69:
70:              :param df_posts: DataFrame with social media posts
71:              :param client: OpenAI client instance
72:              :return: DataFrame with added classification column
73:              """
74:
75:              docs = df_posts.post_text.tolist()
76:              for doc in docs:
77:                  messages = generate_classification_prompt(doc)
78:                  result = get_model_response(messages, client)
79:                  df_posts.loc[
80:                      df_posts["post_text"] == doc,
81:                      "classification"
82:                  ] = result
83:              return df_posts
84:
85:
86:              # Load environment variables and retrieve OpenAI API key
87:              load_dotenv()
88:              api_key = os.getenv("OPENAI_API_KEY")
```

(continued)

(continued)

```
89:      if not api_key:
90:          raise ValueError(
91:              "OPENAI_API_KEY not found in environment
             variables or.env file"
92:          )
93:      # Initialize OpenAI client
94:      client = OpenAI(api_key=api_key)
95:
96:      # Load social media posts from CSV file
97:      df_posts = pd.read_csv(csv_path)
98:
99:      # Assign classifications to posts making calls to OpenAI
         GPT model
100:     df_posts = assign_classification(df_posts, client)
101:
102:     # Set pandas option to display full text of posts in
         DataFrame
103:     pd.set_option("display.max_colwidth", None)
104:
105:     # Display the DataFrame with classifications
106:     display(df_posts)
107:
108:     # Save the DataFrame with classifications to a Parquet
         file
109:     df_posts.to_parquet(parquet_path, index=False)
```

Lines 12 to 42 define the generate_classification_prompt() function, which generates the messages required by the OpenAI Chat API to classify a social media post. Lines 24 to 27 and 28 to 37 define the system and user prompts. The user prompt indicates that a social media post delimited by the content of the delimiter variable ("###") is provided. It instructs the model to identify the main class of the post as "self-promotion", "ingratiation", or "supplication" and to output only one of these words or the word "None" if the post does not fit any of the classes. Line 36 embeds the social media post into the message, which is surrounded by the "###" string. Lines 38 to 41 create a list of messages with the system and user prompts, and line 42 returns the list.

Lines 45 to 60 implement the get_model_response() function, which sends the messages to the OpenAI API and then extracts and returns the response. Only the model and messages required parameters are passed to the chat.completions.create() API function.

If needed, optional parameters, such as `temperature` and `top_p`, explained in Chapter 2, can be passed to the function. The response from the API call is stored in the `result` variable.

Lines 63 to 83 define the `assign_classification()` function, which generates the classification for each post contained in the dataframe passed as input. Line 75 extracts the text of all social media posts from the `'post_text'` column of the input `df_posts` dataframe and converts them into a list of strings named `docs`. Lines 76 to 82 implement a for loop over the posts in the `docs` list. For each of them, line 77 generates the messages for the API, and line 78 retrieves the model's response to those messages. Lines 79 to 82 assign the classification result to a new column called "classification" in the original `df_posts` dataframe. The Pandas' loc function is used to ensure that the classification is placed in the correct row corresponding to the processed `doc`.

Lines 87 to 94 execute functions to retrieve the `OPENAI_API_KEY` key and create the API client, while line 97 loads the social media posts from the `../data/All_Synthetic_Data.csv` file in the `data` directory into a Pandas dataframe named `df_posts`.

Line 100 executes the `assign_classification()` function that adds the `classification` column to the `df_posts` dataframe.

Finally, line 101 sets the `display.max_colwidth` Pandas option to display the full text of posts, line 106 displays the dataframe, and line 109 saves the dataframe in parquet format to a file named `All_Synthetic_Data_with_zero_shot.parquet` in the same data directory. This is needed to retrieve the results of the classification later for analysis.

Figure 8.3 shows the first and last lines of the dataframe, with the "classification" column added.

One-Shot Classification

In one-shot classification, to improve performance, we add descriptions of each IM behavior as an additional context in the prompt. We follow the literature on IM behaviors to define each of them briefly. The code is the same as in the zero-shot example, except for the content of the `user_message` variable in lines 33 to 36, which define the IM categories. Since that is the only difference, the following code only shows the new `user_message`. The complete code of this example is available in the `one_shot_classification_IM_gpt.ipynb` notebook and in the HTML file with the LLM-generated explanations.

post_id	owner	post_date	post_text	classification
0	1	Clean Lady	2023-11-01	🌑 As a climate activist, every day feels like …	None
1	2	Clean Lady	2023-11-02	Recycling isn't just about bins and labels—it'…	None
2	3	Clean Lady	2023-11-03	🌱 Excited to announce that I'm collaborating w…	self-promotion
3	4	Clean Lady	2023-11-04	🌑 Did you know that recycling one aluminum can…	self-promotion
4	5	Clean Lady	2023-11-05	As climate change accelerates, so does my pass…	None
…	…	…	…	…	…
1110	1111	Student-m	2023-11-25	In talking to fellow students, I recognize a s…	None
1111	1112	Student-m	2023-11-26	Events like idea labs and hackathons encourage…	None
1112	1113	Student-m	2023-11-27	I've been reflecting on the role of education …	None
1113	1114	Student-m	2023-11-28	Art has a powerful ability to foster connectio…	None
1114	1115	Student-m	2023-11-29	Closing out November with gratitude for the co…	ingratiation

Fig. 8.3 Classification output from the zero_shot_classification_IM_gpt.ipynb notebook

```
25:             user_message = f"""
26:                 Below is a social media post delimited with
            {delimiter}.
27:                 Identify the main category of this post as
            either
28:                 self-promotion, ingratiation, or
            supplication.
29:
30:                 Definition of categories:
31:                 Self-promotion highlights accomplishments and
            competence.
32:                 Ingratiation praises others.
33:                 Supplication shows limitations.
34:
35:                 Output only the word "self-promotion",
            "ingratiation" or
36:                 "supplication".
37:                 If post is none of these, return the word
            "None".
38:
39:                 Social media post:
            {delimiter}{doc}{delimiter}
40:             """
```

Few-Shot Classification

Few-shot classification further instructs the model with examples and the desired output. The prompt aims to provide context and guidance with concrete examples to improve the model's performance. In the example below, the prompt has three examples, one for each possible outcome of the classification, signaling the expected output. As such, this necessitates a small labeled data sample for crafting the prompt. These labeled samples need to be carefully reviewed by the researcher to ensure that they are consistent with the theoretical framework of the project. The code for this example is available in the few_shot_classification_IM_gpt.ipynb notebook. An LLM-generated description of the code is available in the few_shot_classification_IM_gpt.html file. The code is the same as in the zero and one-shot classification examples, except for the user_message string, which is shown below.

```
26:        user_message = f""""
27:            Below is a social media post delimited with
{delimiter}.
28:            Identify the main category of this post as either
29:            self-promotion, ingratiation, or supplication.
30:
31:            Definition of categories:
32:            Self-promotion highlights accomplishments and
competence.
33:            Ingratiation praises others.
34:            Supplication shows limitations.
35:
36:            Examples:
37:            Example 1: I'm thrilled to have shared my experience
at the
38:            Mission Driven Innovation Event yesterday :-)
Exactly one
39:         .  year ago, I was a participant, and now I'm an
'inspirer'. It's
40:            a crazy feeling!
41:            Answer 1: Self-promotion
42:            Example 2: Congratulations to my sponsor and young
ambassador
43:            coach for his advice. During our first meeting, he
told me:
44:            "We are going to win a prize." Winning bet.
45:            Answer 2: Ingratiation
46:            Example 3: I'm so proud to have been part of this
episode and
47:            taken on the challenge of truly opening up. I
couldn't have
48:            done it without her kindness and positivity! To talk
about
49:            success is more than just listing achievements. It's
about
50:            sharing your journey, values, and the tough times
when you
51:            feel overwhelmed. Being an entrepreneur isn't all
sunshine
52:            and rainbows (not just LinkedIn posts #successful).
For those
53:            listening, this wasn't easy for me. I've always
struggled
54:            with sharing personal things, and I'm not the best at
pitching.
55:            Answer 3: Supplication
```

(continued)

(continued)

```
56:
57:             Output only the word "self-promotion",
        "ingratiation" or
58:                "supplication".
59:                If post is none of these, return the word "None".
60:
61:                Social media post: {delimiter}{doc}{delimiter}
62:       """
```

In this section, we delved into how to use different types of models for classification tasks. From open-source fine-tuned models to proprietary models, LLMs' capabilities in classification are extensive. They can be adapted to a vast number of research projects. However, LLMs must be applied cautiously, as these models are based on probabilistic methods, and the outputs are tied to their training data and parameters. Moreover, their stochastic nature incorporates randomness in their responses, resulting in different answers in each iteration. Therefore, in the following section, we discuss several considerations when implementing these models in classification tasks.

CONSIDERATIONS WHEN USING LLMs AS CLASSIFIERS

The three previous examples show that for the same task of classifying 1115 posts into domain-specific categories, the output can vary significantly depending on the prompt design. Zero-shot classification, which utilizes the model's general training without additional examples, assigned one of the three class labels to 326 posts (29.2% of the total). In comparison, when the one-shot classification prompt, which incorporates a description to guide the model, was used, the number of posts with one of the three classes assigned increased to 530 (47.5% of the total). This additional context helped the model find more posts aligned with the specified criteria. The use of the few-shot classification prompt, which includes examples of the expected outcome, resulted in only 166 posts being assigned to one of the three classes (14.8% of the total). This shows that using a prompt with more detailed criteria can, a priori, produce a more accurate classification. However, it can leave multiple posts unclassified since they do not meet the more detailed criteria. Therefore, providing more context in the prompt does not necessarily translate to better classification outcomes. Moreover, these results are based on a single execution of each prompt. As more executions are performed, variation in the resulting classifications may occur. Multiple executions of the three prompts may be needed to generate a reliable classification (Tai et al., 2024).

These results underscore the need for the cautious application of LLMs as classifiers. While LLMs offer versatile capabilities for data classification, their application must be tempered with a thorough understanding of their limitations. They can offer fast and valuable results but simultaneously introduce variability in the output as a result of differences in the prompt and their stochastic nature. Failing to account for these limitations, the reliability and validity of classifications can be compromised.

To improve the reliability of the classification, researchers can use validation techniques commonly employed in supervised learning, adapted for LLMs. For example, a large labeled data sample can be created as ground truth to measure the accuracy of the classification outputs produced by different prompts across several executions. This requires manually labeling a considerable amount of data and then evaluating the classifications. Thus, researchers should carefully evaluate the benefits and limitations of LLMs within the specific context of their research.

Due to the variations in outputs, LLMs should be viewed as a complementary tool for inductive qualitative research rather than infallible classifiers. Garcia Quevedo et al. (2025) advocated using LLMs as an aid for selecting relevant data when dealing with large datasets, approaching their classification capabilities as preselectors of relevant data rather than as fixed categories for qualitative analysis. Through such classification-based selection, LLMs can enable qualitative researchers to focus on the most relevant data, thereby enhancing qualitative analysis. By integrating LLMs with other NLP techniques and aligning their use with specific research needs, scholars can harness their strengths while mitigating the risks arising from their limitations, thereby advancing their methodological rigor and analytical depth.

Furthermore, we advocate testing various classification techniques using different LLMs. Establishing and well-testing fine-tuned LLMs for NLP tasks such as sentiment analysis, backed by robust research, can improve the reliability of the output. Integrating flexible techniques, such as shot classification, with tested classifiers can improve the robustness of the research design, providing a more comprehensive toolkit for data classification. Each classification technique inherently possesses distinct advantages and limitations. Researchers need to adopt a balanced approach and select methods that best align with their specific objectives and the nature of their data.

REFERENCES

Barbieri, F., Espinosa-Anke, L., & Camacho-Collados, J. (2022). XLM-T: Multilingual language models in Twitter for sentiment analysis and beyond. *Proceedings of the LREC, Marseille, France*, 20–25. https://doi.org/10.48550/arXiv.2104.12250

Camacho-collados, J., Rezaee, K., Riahi, T., Ushio, A., Loureiro, D., Antypas, D., Boisson, J., Espinosa Anke, L., Liu, F., & Martínez Cámara, E. (2022). TweetNLP: Cutting-edge natural language processing for social media. In W. Che & E. Shutova (Eds.), *Proceedings of the 2022 conference on empirical methods in natural language processing: system demonstrations* (pp. 38–49). Association for Computational Linguistics. https://doi.org/10.18653/v1/2022.emnlp-demos.5

Charmaz, K., & Thornberg, R. (2021). The pursuit of quality in grounded theory. *Qualitative Research in Psychology, 18*(3), 305–327. https://doi.org/10.1080/14780887.2020.1780357

Garcia Quevedo, D., Glaser, A., & Verzat, C. (2025). Enhancing theorization using artificial intelligence: Leveraging large language models for qualitative analysis of online data. *Organizational Research Methods 29*(1), 92–112. https://doi.org/10.1177/10944281251339144

Grodal, S., Anteby, M., & Holm, A. L. (2021). Achieving rigor in qualitative analysis: The role of active categorization in theory building. *Academy of Management Review, 46*(3), 591–612. https://doi.org/10.5465/amr.2018.0482

Jones, E., & Pittman, T. (1982). Toward a general theory of strategic self-presentation. In J. Suis (Ed.), *Psychological perspectives on the self* (Vol. 1, pp. 231–262). Lawrence Erlbaum Associates Publishers.

Lewis, M., Liu, Y., Goyal, N., Ghazvininejad, M., Mohamed, A., Levy, O., Stoyanov, V., & Zettlemoyer, L. (2019). BART: Denoising sequence-to-sequence pre-training for natural language generation, translation, and comprehension. arXiv:1910.13461. https://doi.org/10.48550/arXiv.1910.13461

Ouyang, L., Wu, J., Jiang, X., Almeida, D., Wainwright, C. L., Mishkin, P., Zhang, C., Agarwal, S., Slama, K., Ray, A., Schulman, J., Hilton, J., Kelton, F., Miller, L., Simens, M., Askell, A., Welinder, P., Christiano, P., Leike, J., & Lowe, R. (2022). Training language models to follow instructions with human feedback. *Advances in Neural Information Processing Systems*, 27730–27744.

Saldaña, J. (2013). *The coding manual for qualitative researchers* (2nd ed.). Sage.

Tai, R. H., Bentley, L. R., Xia, X., Sitt, J. M., Fankhauser, S. C., Chicas-Mosier, A. M., & Monteith, B. G. (2024). An examination of the use of large language models to aid analysis of textual data. *International Journal of Qualitative Methods, 23*, 16094069241231168. https://doi.org/10.1177/16094069241231168

Yin, W., Hay, J., & Roth, D. (2019). Benchmarking zero-shot text classification: Datasets, evaluation and entailment approach. arXiv:1909.00161. https://doi.org/10.48550/arXiv.1909.00161

CHAPTER 9

Clustering and Topic Modeling

Abstract This chapter presents clustering and topic modeling as important techniques in natural language processing (NLP) for qualitative research. It highlights topic modeling as a specialized form of clustering aimed at uncovering hidden thematic structures within text datasets. Large language models (LLMs) improve the interpretability and coherence of topics compared with traditional methods. This chapter also addresses limitations such as topic instability and model hallucinations. Practical code examples illustrate the implementation of topic generation and assignment, thereby fostering a deeper understanding of the applicability of this NLP task in qualitative analysis.

Keywords Topic modeling · Natural language processing · Large language models

Clustering is a well-established NLP task that groups similar documents, text segments, or words on the basis of similarity criteria. The data points in a cluster are more similar to each other than to those in other clusters. Clustering is an inductive technique that does not require training on labeled data. It identifies natural groupings or clusters of data points within the text. Topic modeling is a specialized clustering technique that aims to discover the underlying thematic structure in a collection of texts without requiring predefined labels, classification, or training data.

© The Author(s) 2026
D. Garcia Quevedo and J. Kuri, *AI for Qualitative Research*,
https://doi.org/10.1007/978-3-032-08872-7_9

Topic modeling is widely used in management research and other domains to find implicit topics in datasets (Hannigan et al., 2019; Schmiedel et al., 2019). Understanding the themes or topics in a collection of texts is valuable in data analysis, and for this reason, topic modeling has been widely developed over the years. Traditional topic modeling algorithms such as latent Dirichlet allocation (LDA) rely on word-level counts and statistics. However, these algorithms fail to capture the semantic structure of sentences, paragraphs, and entire documents. LLMs excel at capturing the nuance of human language, making them especially useful for topic modeling (Egger & Yu, 2022).

Understanding Topic Modeling with LLMs

With their ability to capture nuanced semantic relationships between words, sentences, and paragraphs, LLMs provide advantages over traditional topic modeling methods. These include not only more coherent and interpretable topics but also the ability to identify complex and nuanced topics, particularly in domains with jargon or specialized language (Bhaduri et al., 2024; Kapoor et al., 2024). These qualities improve the discovery and understanding of underlying topics in large datasets.

However, as mentioned in previous chapters, LLMs have limitations that need to be considered when implementing a topic modeling task. One limitation is topic instability, which refers to models producing a different set of topics in each execution. Another is the risk of producing nonexistent topics that appear to be real because of model hallucinations (Spielberger et al., 2025). A third limitation is the risk of models failing to retrieve topics present in the data. A fourth limitation is the risk of model bias reflected in the output. Researchers should address these limitations systematically. Python programs provide an efficient way to explore and evaluate topic modeling tasks by implementing variations in prompts, models, and other factors.

Leveraging Topic Modeling for Data Analysis

The approach to topic modeling with LLMs described in this section consists of two steps: topic generation and topic assignment. In the first step, a prompt is created containing the text of the input dataset (e.g., social media posts) and instructions for the model to return the set of main topics present in it, along with a brief description of each topic. Optionally, the prompt can indicate how many topics need to be returned. The second step, topic assignment, involves assigning the most relevant topics from the generated list to each item in the input dataset. An item may be assigned zero, one, or more topics. Optionally, the prompt can indicate the exclusive assignment of one topic to each input item. In some cases, the model will not assign any topics to a post. This may occur if the post lacks sufficient information, such as a post with only a few words with no particular message. It can also occur if the text does not match any of the generated topics. Since the model determines what the main topics are, its list is not guaranteed to be exhaustive.

The code also includes functionality to generate subtopics. This is implemented by iterating over the topics defined in the first two steps. For each topic, subtopics are generated and assigned to the posts belonging to the topic. The code for this example is available in the `topic_modeling_gemini.ipynb` notebook. The LLM-generated description is available in the `topic_modeling_gemini.html` file.

The code implements a complete topic modeling system that intends to be comprehensive and adaptable to different topic modeling tasks. The code consists of the following main sections: (1) importing of libraries and definition of global settings; (2) definition of the data structure representing a topic and its description; (3) implementation of a `generate_topic_generation_prompt()` function that constructs the prompt instructing the LLM to generate topics from a list of posts; (4) implementation of a `generate_topics_dataframe()` function that generates a list of topics and their descriptions; (5) implementation of a `generate_topic_assignment_prompt()` function that creates the prompt for the LLM to assign predefined topics to social media posts; (6) implementation of an `assign_topics()` function that uses an LLM to assign topics to posts, processing the posts in blocks; (7) a main execution block that initializes a Gemini API client, loads the data, generates and assigns topics, and saves the results; and (8) implementation of subtopic generation and assignment within the main execution block that generates and assigns subtopics for each primary topic, then saves the results.

Due to the extent of the code, this has been divided into several blocks to facilitate its explanation. For brevity, only the new lines of code are explained in detail.

The following code contains the first two sections: importing libraries, defining global settings, and defining the data structure representing a topic and its description.

```
 1:    # Import libraries
 2:    import os
 3:    import re
 4:    import pandas as pd
 5:    from google import genai
 6:    from pydantic import BaseModel
 7:    from dotenv import load_dotenv
 8:    from IPython.display import display
 9:
10:    # Set pandas option to display full text of posts in DataFrame
11:    pd.set_option("display.max_colwidth", None)
12:    # Set pandas option to display all rows in DataFrame
13:    pd.set_option('display.max_rows', None)
14:
15:
16:    # Define a model for the topic structure
17:    class Topic(BaseModel):
18:        topic_name: str
19:        topic_description: str
```

Lines 17 to 19 define a Python class with the expected structure of a topic: a topic name and a topic description. This class is used in the call to indicate to the LLM the structure that the generated topics must have.

The following part of the code contains section 3: implementation of the `generate_topic_generation_prompt()` function that constructs the prompt instructing the LLM to generate topics from a list of posts.

```
22:    def generate_topic_generation_prompt(docs, num_
       topics=None):
23:        """Generate a prompt for topic modeling of posts.
24:
25:        Creates a prompt for Gemini API to find main topics in
           posts.
26:        Formats posts with delimiters. Requests JSON response
           with topic
27:        names and descriptions.
28:
```

(continued)

(continued)

```
29:        :param docs: List of post texts to analyze
30:        :return: Messages for Gemini API with structure:
31:            [
32:                    {"role": "system", "content": str},
33:                    {"role": "user", "content": str}
34:            ]
35:        """
36:        topic_count = "" if num_topics is None else num_
       topics
37:        delimiter = "###"
38:        system_message = """
39:            You're a helpful assistant.
40:            Your task is to analyze social media posts.
41:        """
42:        user_message = f"""
43:            Below is a set of social media posts delimited
44:            with {delimiter}.
45:            Identify the main {topic_count} topics mentioned
       in these
46:            comments and provide a brief description of each
       topic.
47:            Topics must be as distinct from each other as
       possible and
48:            cover as many different aspects of the posts as
       possible.
49:            Output is in JSON format.
50:
51:            Social media posts:
52:            {delimiter}
53:            {delimiter.join(docs)}
54:            {delimiter}
55:        """
56:
57:        return [
58:            {"role": "system", "content": system_message},
59:            {"role": "user", "content": user_message},
60:        ]
```

In line 36, if the optional num_topics parameter is provided, the value of that parameter is added to the user_message string to indicate to the LLM the number of topics to generate. The rest of the function is similar to the prompt generation functions in the previous chapters.

The following part of the code contains section 4: implementation of the `generate_topics_dataframe()` function that generates a list of topics and their descriptions.

```
63:        def generate_topics_dataframe(
64:            df_posts,
65:            client,
66:            model,
67:            num_topics=None,
68:            post_text_column="post_text"
69:        ):
70:            """Create DataFrame with topics and descriptions
               from posts.

71:
72:            Takes posts DataFrame, uses Gemini API to identify
               topics,
73:            returns DataFrame with topics and descriptions.
74:
75:            :param df_posts: DataFrame with posts
76:            :param post_text_column: Name of column with text
77:            :return: DataFrame with ["topic", "description"]
               columns
78:            :raises ValueError: If post_text_column not found
               in df_posts
79:            """
80:            if post_text_column not indf_posts.columns:
81:                raise ValueError(
82:                    f"Column '{post_text_column}' not found in
               DataFrame."
83:                )
84:
85:            # Get list of posts from DataFrame
86:            docs = df_posts[post_text_column].tolist()
87:
88:            # Generate prompt messages
89:            messages = generate_topic_generation_prompt(docs,
               num_topics)
90:
91:            # Generate topics using Gemini API
92:            response = client.models.generate_content(
93:                model=model,
94:                contents=messages[1]["content"],
95:                config={
96:                    "response_mime_type": "application/json",
97:                    "response_schema": list[Topic],
98:                },
```

(continued)

(continued)

```
 99:            )
100:
101:            # Convert response to DataFrame
102:            df_topics = pd.DataFrame(
103:                [
104:                    {
105:                        "topic_name": topic.topic_name,
106:                        "topic_description": topic.topic_
        description
107:                    }
108:                    for topic in response.parsed
109:                ]
110:            )
111:
112:            return df_topics
```

Lines 80 to 83 verify if the `"post_text"` column exists in the dataframe. Line 86 converts the posts in the `"post_text"` column into a list of strings. Line 89 calls the `generate_topic_generation_prompt()` function explained above. Lines 92 to 99 make the API call to the model. The user prompt is passed in the `contents` parameter (line 94). Lines 95 to 98 define the value of the `config` parameter, a Python dictionary that specifies that the response must be in JSON format, and adhere to the `list[Topic]` schema (the topic class is defined in lines 17 to 19). Finally, lines 102 to 110 convert the response of the model into a Pandas dataframe.

The following contains section 5: implementation of the `generate_topic_assignment_prompt()` function, which creates the prompt for the LLM to assign predefined topics to social media posts.

```
115:        def generate_topic_assignment_prompt(
116:            df_posts,
117:            df_topics,
118:            topic_name_column
119:        ):
120:            """Create prompt to assign topics to posts.
121:
122:            Makes prompt for Gemini API to assign topics from
        predefined list
123:            to posts. Uses delimiters for topics and posts,
        with instructions
```

(continued)

124:	*for matching.*
125:	
126:	*:param df_posts: DataFrame with 'post_text' column*
127:	*:param df_topics: DataFrame with topic_name_ column*
128:	*:return: Messages for Gemini API:*
129:	*[*
130:	*{"role": "system", "content": str},*
131:	*{"role": "user", "content": str}*
132:	*]*
133:	`""""`
134:	`topics_delimiter = "%%%"`
135:	`posts_delimiter = "###"`
136:	`system_message = """`
137:	You're a helpful assistant. Your task is to analyze social
138:	media posts and assign them to topics.
139:	`"""`
140:	`user_message = f"""`
141:	Below is a set of topics delimited with {topics_delimiter}
142:	and a set of social media posts delimited
143:	with {posts_delimiter}.
144:	Identify for each post the list of topics that it belongs to.
145:	Only topics from the provided set of topics can be used.
146:	If a post does not belong to any of the provided topics,
147:	return for that post a list with a single item "None".
148:	Return the results in JSON format.
149:	
150:	Topics:
151:	{topics_delimiter}
152:	{topics_delimiter.join(df_topics[topic_name_ column].tolist())}
153:	{topics_delimiter}
154:	
155:	Social media posts:
156:	{posts_delimiter}
157:	{posts_delimiter.join(df_posts["post_ text"].tolist())}
158:	{posts_delimiter}
159:	`"""`

(continued)

(continued)

```
160:
161:        return [
162:            {"role": "system", "content": system_
            message},
163:            {"role": "user", "content": user_message},
164:        ]
```

The posts and topics are passed in the df_posts and df_topics input parameters, respectively. The function creates the system and user messages. In the latter, the posts are embedded into messages, delimited by "###" as well as the topics, delimited by the "%%%" string.

The following part of the code contains section 6: Implementation of the assign_topics() function, which uses an LLM to assign topics to posts, processing the posts one block at a time.

```
167:    def assign_topics(
168:            df_posts,
169:            df_topics,
170:            client,
171:            model,
172:            topic_name_column,
173:            assigned_topics_column,
174:            block_size=100,
175:    ):
176:        """Assign topics and optionally subtopics to social
        media posts.
177:
178:        This function takes DataFrames containing posts and
        topics, uses
179:        the Gemini API to analyze each post, and assigns
        relevant topics
180:        from the provided topic list. If subtopics are
        provided, it also
181:        assigns relevant subtopics for each assigned topic.
182:        It processes posts in blocks to handle larger datasets
        efficiently.
183:
184:        :param df_posts: posts DataFrame with a 'post_text'
        column
185:        :param df_topics: DataFrame with topic_name_column
186:        :param client: Initialized Gemini API client
187:        :param model: Name of the Gemini model to use
```

(continued)

(continued)

188:	*:param block_size: Number of posts to process in each batch*
189:	*:return: Input DataFrame with assigned_topics_column added*
190:	*""""*
191:	*# Create a copy to avoid modifying the input DataFrame*
192:	df_result = df_posts.copy().reset_index(drop=**True**)
193:	df_result[assigned_topics_column] = **None**
194:	*# if df_subtopics is not None:*
195:	*# df_result["subtopics"] = None*
196:	
197:	*# Process posts in blocks*
198:	**for** start_idx **in** range(0, len(df_posts), block_size):
199:	end_idx = min(start_idx + block_size, len(df_posts))
200:	df_block = df_posts.iloc[start_idx:end_idx]
201:	
202:	print(f"\nProcessing posts {start_idx} to {end_idx-1}...")
203:	
204:	*# Generate prompt for the current block*
205:	messages = generate_topic_assignment_prompt(
206:	df_block,
207:	df_topics,
208:	topic_name_column
209:	)
210:	
211:	*# Get model response for topic assignment*
212:	response = client.models.generate_content(
213:	model=model,
214:	contents=messages[1]["content"],
215:	config={
216:	"response_mime_type": "application/json",
217:	"response_schema": list[list[str]],
218:	},
219:	)
220:	
221:	*# Assign topics to the current block*
222:	**for** i, topics **in** enumerate(response.parsed):
223:	print(f"Post {start_idx + i}: Topics assigned: {topics}")
224:	df_result.at[start_idx + i, assigned_topics_column] = (

(continued)

(continued)

225:	`"   |   ".join(topics)`
226:	`)`
227:	
228:	`print(f"Assigned topics to {end_idx-start_idx} posts.")`
229:	
230:	`return df_result`

Line 193 adds to the dataframe a new column that will contain the list of topics assigned to each post and initializes it with None. Lines 198 to 228 iterate through the posts in blocks whose size is defined by the block_size parameter. Lines 199 and 200 calculate the start and end indices of the current block and create a sub-dataframe with only those rows. Lines 205 to 209 call the generate_topic_assignment_ prompt() function described above, and lines 212 to 219 call the API function that sends the prompt to the LLM. The config parameter in lines 215 to 218 indicates that the result must be returned in JSON format and must be a list of lists. Each of these lists inside the main list represents the set of topics assigned to each post. Lines 222 to 226 assign the topics to the records in the df_result dataframe.

The following contains section 7: the main execution block initializes a Gemini API client, loads the data, generates and assigns topics, and saves the results.

233:	`# Load environment variables and get API key`
234:	`load_dotenv()`
235:	`api_key = os.getenv("GEMINI_API_KEY")`
236:	`if not api_key:`
237:	`raise ValueError(`
238:	`"Missing GEMINI_API_KEY in environment or .env file"`
239:	`)`
240:	`client = genai.Client(api_key=api_key)`
241:	
242:	`model = "gemini-2.5-flash"`
243:	
244:	`# Read social media posts from CSV file`
245:	`df_posts = pd.read_csv("../data/All_Synthetic_ Data.csv")`
246:	`# DEBUG: Use a small sample for testing`

(continued)

(continued)

```
247:    # df_posts = df_posts.sample(
248:    #     100,
249:    #     random_state=42
250:    # ).reset_index(drop=True)
251:
252:    # Generate topics from posts
253:    df_topics = generate_topics_dataframe(df_posts, client,
        model)
254:
255:    # Assign topics to posts
256:    df_posts = assign_topics(
257:        df_posts,
258:        df_topics,
259:        client,
260:        model,
261:        topic_name_column="topic_name",
262:        assigned_topics_column="assigned_topics",
263:        block_size=50,
264:        # df_subtopics=df_subtopics
265:    )
266:
267:    print("Identified Topics:")
268:    display(df_topics)
269:
270:    print("Posts with assigned topics:")
271:    display(df_posts)
272:    # Save results to parquet files
273:    df_topics.to_parquet(
274:        "topic_modeling_gemini_topics.parquet",
275:        index=False
276:    )
277:    df_posts.to_parquet(
278:        "topic_modeling_gemini_posts.parquet",
279:        index=False
280:    )
```

Lines 234 to 245 implement the same functionality as in the previous code examples. Line 253 calls the generate_topics_dataframe() function described above and assigns the result to the df_topics variable, which is a dataframe containing the list of topics and their descriptions. Lines 256 to 265 call the assign_topics() function and assign the result to the df_posts variable. Lines 268 and 271 display the content of the df_topics and df_posts dataframes, and lines 273 to 280 save the dataframes to parquet files.

The following part of the code contains section 8: implementation of subtopic generation and assignment within the main execution block that generates and assigns subtopics for each primary topic and then saves the results.

```
283:    total_matches = 0
284:    df_subtopics_all = pd.DataFrame()
285:    df_posts_with_subtopics = pd.DataFrame()
286:
287:    # Generate subtopics for each topic
288:    for topic in df_topics["topic_name"].tolist():
289:        print(f"Topic: {topic}")
290:        m = df_posts["assigned_topics"].str.contains(
291:            re.escape(topic),
292:            na=False
293:        )
294:        df_posts_topic_subset = df_posts[m]
295:        total_matches += (matches := len(df_posts_topic_
       subset))
296:        print(f"Number of posts assigned to this topic:
       {matches}")
297:        df_subtopics = generate_topics_dataframe(
298:        df_posts_topic_subset,
299:            client,
300:            model
301:        )
302:        df_subtopics = df_subtopics.rename(
303:            columns={
304:                "topic_name": "subtopic_name",
305:                "topic_description": "subtopic_description"
306:            }
307:        )
308:        df_subtopics["topic_name"] = topic
309:        # Assign df_subtopics to the filtered posts
310:        df_tmp = assign_topics(
311:            df_posts_topic_subset,
312:            df_subtopics,
313:            client,
314:            model,
315:            topic_name_column="subtopic_name",
316:            assigned_topics_column="assigned_subtopics",
317:            block_size=50,
318:        )
```

(continued)

(continued)

```
319:        df_posts_with_subtopics = pd.concat(
320:            [df_posts_with_subtopics, df_tmp],
321:            ignore_index=True
322:        )
323:        df_subtopics_all = pd.concat(
324:            [df_subtopics_all, df_subtopics],
325:            ignore_index=True
326:        )
327:
328:        print(f"Total posts assigned to topics: {total_matches}")
329:
330:        # Coalesce into a single column subtopics for posts with
            multiple topics
331:        df_posts_with_subtopics = df_posts_with_
            subtopics.groupby(
332:            df_posts.columns.to_list()
333:        )["assigned_subtopics"].agg(lambda x: ' |
            '.join(x)).reset_index()
334:
335:        # Add posts that were not assigned any topics
336:        df_posts_with_subtopics = pd.concat(
337:            [df_posts_with_subtopics, df_posts[df_posts.assigned_
            topics=="None"]],
338:            ignore_index=True
339:        )
340:        df_posts_with_subtopics.assigned_subtopics = (
341:            df_posts_with_subtopics.assigned_
            subtopics.fillna("None")
342:        )
343:        # Merge topics and subtopics into a single DataFrame
344:        df_subtopics = pd.merge(
345:            df_topics,
346:            df_subtopics_all,
347:            on="topic_name",
348:            how="left"
349:        )
350:
351:        # Save topics, subtopics, and posts with subtopics to
            parquet files
352:        df_subtopics.to_parquet(
353:            "topic_modeling_gemini_subtopics.parquet",
354:            index=False
355:        )
356:        df_posts_with_subtopics.to_parquet(
```

(continued)

(continued)

```
357:        "topic_modeling_gemini_posts_with_
            subtopics.parquet",
358:            index=False
359:    )
360:
361:    print("Identified topics & subtopics:")
362:    display(df_subtopics)
363:
364:    print("Posts with assigned topics and subtopics:")
365:    display(df_posts_with_subtopics)
```

Lines 284 and 285 initialize dataframes that store the generated subtopics and the posts with their assigned subtopics. Lines 288 to 326 implement a for loop that iterates over the list of unique topics generated in the previous steps. For each topic, the subset of posts with that topic assigned is assigned to the df_posts_topic_subset variable. Lines 297 to 318 use the generate_topics_dataframe() and assign_topics() functions described above to generate and assign subtopics to this subset of posts. Lines 319 to 326 append the generated subtopics and assignments-to-posts to the df_subtopics_all and df_posts_with_subtopics dataframes. Lines 331 to 333 combine the different subtopics assigned to each post into a single string and assign it to the "assigned_subtopics" column of the dataframe. Lines 336 to 342 add to the df_posts_with_subtopics dataframe posts that were not assigned any subtopic, and lines 344 to 349 combine the df_topics and df_subtopics_all dataframes into a single dataframe. Lines 352 to 359 save the dataframes into parquet files, and lines 362 and 365 display their contents.

Figure 9.1 shows the outputs of lines 267 to 271. For brevity, only the first three posts are shown.

Considerations of Topic Modeling for Qualitative Analysis

Topic modeling leveraging LLMs presents several benefits for qualitative researchers. One significant advantage lies in the efficiency and scalability of LLMs. Owing to their capacity to rapidly process vast amounts of text, LLMs can significantly accelerate the initial stages of identifying

```
Identified Topics:
```

	topic_name	topic_description
0	Environmental Sustainability and Recycling	Focuses on efforts and innovations aimed at protecting the environment, including waste reduction, promoting recycling, fostering a circular economy, and engaging communities in sustainable practices to combat climate change.
1	Financial Technology (FinTech) and Social Impact	Explores the transformative role of technology in financial services, focusing on innovations like AI and blockchain, while also addressing crucial aspects of financial inclusion, literacy, cybersecurity, ethical practices, and sustainable investments.
2	Diversity, Equity, and Inclusion (DEI) in STEM & Workplace	Highlights the importance of fostering diverse, equitable, and inclusive environments within STEM fields and professional workplaces, addressing challenges faced by underrepresented groups, and emphasizing mentorship, advocacy, and supportive workplace cultures.
3	Healthcare Innovation and Women's Health	Covers advancements and challenges in the medical field, particularly in women's health, including technological innovations like telemedicine and AI, the critical importance of mental health, patient education, health equity, and policy advocacy.
4	Art, Politics, and Social Justice	Examines the powerful intersection of artistic expression, political discourse, and social justice, highlighting how art can serve as a tool for activism, cultural representation, and community engagement to address societal issues and drive change.
5	Energy Policy and Climate Realism	Discusses the complexities of global energy landscapes and climate policy, advocating for a balanced approach to energy sources, acknowledging economic impacts, and promoting critical thinking on environmental narratives beyond singular solutions.

```
Posts with assigned topics:
```

	post_id	owner	post_date	post_text	assigned_topics
0	1	Clean Lady	2023-11-01	🌐 As a climate activist, every day feels like ...	Environmental Sustainability and Recycling
1	2	Clean Lady	2023-11-02	Recycling isn't just about bins and labels—it'...	Environmental Sustainability and Recycling
2	3	Clean Lady	2023-11-03	♻ Excited to announce that I'm collaborating w...	Environmental Sustainability and Recycling

Fig. 9.1 Topic modeling output from the topic_modeling_gemini.ipynb notebook

potential themes, allowing researchers to handle larger corpora more effectively. LLMs can potentially reveal novel and deeper insights by identifying patterns and connections within the data that researchers might inadvertently overlook. They can offer a fresh perspective without the same inherent assumption that researchers may carry, potentially uncovering unexpected themes that might enhance the research findings (Garcia Quevedo et al., 2025).

However, it is crucial to acknowledge the significant limitations of topic generation by LLMs. As previously mentioned, one primary concern revolves around the models' stochastic behavior, which hinders their reliability. Each execution of the above code will generate a different set of topics and descriptions. The prompt can be modified to determine the number of topics. However, variations in the outputs still occur. The topic assignment will also vary, even if the same list of topics is used. Researchers must make decisions through this process. For example, they need to critically decide how many executions are needed, the desired number of topics, and the level of exclusivity in topic assignment. These considerations are essential to ensure robust results.

Another key limitation lies in the lack of interpretability and contextual understanding. While LLMs can identify patterns and relationships in text, they do not possess genuine interpretive capabilities or a human-like understanding. Moreover, they struggle to grasp the subjective meaning, subtle understanding, and contextual factors rich in interpretative research (De Paoli, 2024). As such, the topics generated serve as a starting point but not the culmination of a research project.

Researchers should be cautious about LLMs' hallucinations, which can distort or misinterpret data by incorrectly naming and describing topics on the basis of nonexistent top words (Mu et al., 2024). The risk of producing fabricated information, even with advancements in mitigating hallucinations, can be minimized by critically examining outputs and utilizing multiple models for verification purposes.

Garcia Quevedo et al. (2025) proposed the use of topic modeling as an entry point to select relevant data. They suggest using topic modeling to explore the dataset by understanding the different themes within. They argued that this method enables the researcher to gain a broad understanding of the dataset, provides new insights, and facilitates relevant data selection to enhance manual inductive analysis. However, they do not suggest using topic modeling as a substitute for manual inductive analysis but rather as a tool for selecting relevant data, helping to narrow the focus to specific topics.

To effectively leverage the benefits of LLMs for topic modeling, researchers must implement robust safeguards throughout their research process. This starts by defining an evaluation framework that combines metrics and human assessments (Weston et al., 2023). Examples of metrics typically used to evaluate topic modeling algorithms include topic coherence and topic diversity (Schmiedel et al., 2019). Other aspects to evaluate include the alignment of the produced topics with the provided prompts and the potential presence of bias in the output (Spielberger et al., 2025). Finally, aspects that are difficult to quantify, such as the interpretability and relevance of the generated topics with respect to the research question, also require assessment. As in classification, research oversight and validation are essential. LLMs should be viewed as powerful tools that augment, rather than replace, researchers' critical thinking and interpretive skills (Garcia Quevedo et al., 2025).

Another step that researchers could take to improve the robustness of their analysis is the combination of NLP tasks. In the next chapter, we examine the final NLP task proposed by Garcia Quevedo et al. (2025), which focuses on retrieving specific information via phrases and questions.

REFERENCES

Bhaduri, S., Kapoor, S., Gil, A., Mittal, A., & Mulkar, R. (2024). *Reconciling methodological paradigms: Employing large language models as novice qualitative research assistants in talent management research* (No. arXiv:2408.11043). arXiv. https://doi.org/10.48550/arXiv.2408.11043

De Paoli, S. (2024). Performing an inductive thematic analysis of semi-structured interviews with a large language model: An exploration and provocation on the limits of the approach. *Social Science Computer Review, 42*(4), 997–1019. https://doi.org/10.1177/08944393231220483

Egger, R., & Yu, J. (2022). A topic modeling comparison between LDA, NMF, Top2Vec, and BERTopic to Demystify Twitter Posts. *Frontiers in Sociology, 7*, Article 886498. https://doi.org/10.3389/fsoc.2022.886498

Garcia Quevedo, D., Glaser, A., & Verzat, C. (2025). Enhancing theorization using artificial intelligence: Leveraging large language models for qualitative analysis of online data. *Organizational Research Methods 29*(1), 92–112. https://doi.org/10.1177/10944281251339144

Hannigan, T. R., Haans, R. F., Vakili, K., Tchalian, H., Glaser, V. L., Wang, M. S., Kaplan, S., & Jennings, P. D. (2019). Topic modeling in management research: Rendering new theory from textual data. *Academy of Management Annals*, *13*(2), 586–632.

Kapoor, S., Gil, A., Bhaduri, S., Mittal, A., & Mulkar, R. (2024). *Qualitative insights tool (QualIT): LLM enhanced topic modeling* (No. arXiv:2409.15626). arXiv. https://doi.org/10.48550/arXiv.2409.15626

Mu, Y., Bai, P., Bontcheva, K., & Song, X. (2024). *Addressing topic granularity and hallucination in large language models for topic modelling* (No. arXiv: 2405.00611). arXiv. https://doi.org/10.48550/arXiv.2405.00611

Schmiedel, T., Müller, O., & vom Brocke, J. (2019). Topic modeling as a strategy of inquiry in organizational research: A tutorial with an application example on organizational culture. *Organizational Research Methods*, *22*(4), 941–968. https://doi.org/10.1177/1094428118773858

Spielberger, G., Artinger, F., Reb, J., & Kerschreiter, R. (2025). *Retrieval augmented generation for topic modeling in organizational research: An introduction with empirical demonstration* (No. arXiv:2502.20963). arXiv. https://doi.org/10.48550/arXiv.2502.20963

Weston, S. J., Shryock, I., Light, R., & Fisher, P. A. (2023). Selecting the number and labels of topics in topic modeling: A tutorial. *Advances in Methods and Practices in Psychological Science*, *6*(2), 25152459231160104. https://doi.org/10.1177/25152459231160105

Information Retrieval
and Retrieval-Augmented Generation

Abstract This chapter introduces information retrieval (IR) and retrieval-augmented generation (RAG) as important natural language processing (NLP) tasks for efficiently obtaining relevant information from vast datasets. RAG combines IR with generative capabilities, providing contextually appropriate and factual responses to users' questions. The chapter explains key concepts such as cosine similarity and embeddings, which facilitate nuanced retrieval processes. The chapter presents a practical Python example implementing a simple IR and RAG system, providing guidance for design decisions such as chunk size, model selection, and query crafting.

Keywords Information retrieval · Retrieval-augmented generation · Large language models

In this chapter, we explore information retrieval (IR), an NLP task that has received little attention in management research. IR is a fundamental component for answering questions and search engine systems. IR helps users efficiently find relevant information in vast datasets.

In its simplest form, an IR system matches a user's request with the datasets to which it has access. The user request, referred to as a query, can be anything from a list of keywords to complex paragraphs, videos, or images. The user sends the request to the IR system, which then returns

© The Author(s) 2026   147
D. Garcia Quevedo and J. Kuri, *AI for Qualitative Research*,
https://doi.org/10.1007/978-3-032-08872-7_10

the most relevant data that match the query. It returns a list of retrieved data ranked by their estimated relevance.

Modern IR systems are enhanced with NLP techniques to move beyond simple keyword matching. The systems now analyze the semantics and context of a query to assess the user intent and retrieve information that is conceptually related to the query, even if the returned data do not contain the exact keywords (Spielberger et al., 2025). IR enables access to domain-specific and proprietary information, including research databases, interview transcripts, and other specialized datasets. As such, IR offers new opportunities for qualitative researchers to find relevant data that match their specific research needs.

Modern IR systems integrate the semantic understanding and generative capabilities of LLMs, giving rise to retrieval-augmented generation (RAG). RAG systems consist of two main modules: a retriever and a generative module. First, the retriever module searches a knowledge base, such as a specific set of documents or a research database, to find information relevant to the query. The generative model then incorporates the retrieved information to generate a more accurate, relevant, and factually grounded response. The increasing capacity of LLMs to process longer inputs allows for nuanced and longer queries, providing retrieved information based on shared meaning and enhancing the quality of the generated output.

By generating text from the retrieved information of a knowledge base, RAG systems have the potential to significantly reduce LLMs' key limitations, such as hallucinations and outdated knowledge, i.e., models trained on data available up to a specific cutoff date. This technique allows LLMs to provide up-to-date, contextually appropriate answers on the basis of verifiable data, making them more powerful and reliable (Simon et al., 2024; Spielberger et al., 2025). In the next section, we explore how these LLM-powered techniques work.

Understanding LLM-Based IR and RAG

LLM-based IR and RAG systems rely on two important concepts to account for the nuances of human language in the retrieval process: embedding and cosine similarity.

As explained in Chapter 2, embeddings are representations of complex data such as words, phrases, images, and sounds in a format that computers can understand and use. In the context of NLP, embeddings are created by first breaking words into tokens and then converting each token into a specific list of numbers, called a vector, of length d. The vector is the embedding of the token. Embeddings position tokens in a d-dimensional semantic space where tokens with similar meanings are located close together. LLMs create contextualized embeddings in which the embedding of each token in an input text sequence is refined to become more specific to that input text sequence (Jurafsky & Martin, 2025). For example, the embedding of the word "crane" will differ depending on whether the surrounding text discusses construction or types of birds.

Cosine similarity is a metric used to measure how similar two nonzero vectors are. It measures the cosine of the angle between the two vectors to determine if they point in a similar direction. The values of the metric range from -1 (negative) to 1 (positive). A value of 0 indicates no correlation. Vectors with a cosine similarity of -1 have opposite directions, whereas vectors with a cosine similarity of 1 have identical directions. A cosine similarity close to 1 indicates that the texts associated with the corresponding vectors have a similar meaning. The formula of cosine similarity is as follows:

$$S_c(A, B) = \frac{A \cdot B}{\|A\|\|B\|} = \frac{\sum_{i=1}^{n} A_i B_i}{\sqrt{\sum_{i=1}^{n} A_i^2} \cdot \sqrt{\sum_{i=1}^{n} B_i^2}}$$

where $A \cdot B$ represents the dot product of the vectors and where $\|A\|$ and $\|B\|$ represent the lengths of the vectors. The equation on the right-hand side shows the formulas of the dot product and the vectors' length. In these formulas, A_i and B_i represent the ith components of the A and B vectors, respectively (Jurafsky & Martin, 2025). Cosine similarity is not the only similarity metric, but it is widely used in data analysis.

To illustrate these concepts, let us consider a simple LLM-based IR system. In the system, embeddings are first generated for each item in the dataset (e.g., individual social media posts, sentences, or paragraphs in interview documents) and stored in a file or database. The embeddings are generated only once and do not need to be recomputed in each retrieval operation. To perform a retrieval operation, the embedding of the user's query text is first generated. Then, the cosine similarity is computed for each user query embedding and data item embedding pairing. The data items with the highest cosine similarity are returned since they are semantically closer to the query. Since the embeddings are computed via an LLM, a query and a data item can be semantically close even if they do not have words in common. The simple approach of computing the cosine similarity for all the items in the dataset is practical when the number of items is on the order of thousands, but this approach is no longer viable when the number of items is on the hundreds of thousands or more. In this case, large-scale IR systems rely on advanced indexing, search, and reranking techniques that can trade off accuracy for speed.

The concepts of embeddings and cosine similarity may appear obscure, but it is important to understand them since the performance of the IR and RAG is affected by the embeddings and the similarity metric used.

Specialized open-source libraries such as SentenceTransformers and API functions of proprietary models such as OpenAI's GPT and Google's Gemini can be used to generate embeddings. Examples of how to create embeddings and how to use them in semantic search are available in www.sbert.net, platform.openai.com/docs/guides/embeddings, and ai.google.dev/gemini-api/docs/embeddings. A particular feature of the Gemini API is that embeddings can be created for specific tasks, such as semantic similarity, classification, clustering, document retrieval, query retrieval, code-retrieval-query, question answering, and fact verification. Cosine similarity is a well-established metric in IR and is implemented in popular Python libraries such as sklearn. For convenience, this and other similarity metrics are also implemented in SentenceTransformers, OpenAI (openai.embeddings_utils), and other Python libraries. We use the sklearn implementation in the code examples of this chapter.

USING IR AND RAG

This section uses Python code to explain in practical terms how to perform LLM-based IR and RAG on a set of social media posts. While modern IR and RAG systems can be highly sophisticated and complex, the code provided here is intentionally simple to facilitate comprehension and hands-on experimentation. In particular, the code allows the user to trace what specific posts are passed to the LLM to generate an answer and how those posts were retrieved. This type of visibility is not possible with more sophisticated proprietary services such as Google's NotebookLM, which do not publish their code openly.

We use the same set of 1,115 synthetic social media posts used throughout the book and Google's Gemini embedding model to illustrate the use of task-specific embeddings. The code can be adapted to the specific needs of a project. For example, consider using paragraphs or full documents instead of a single paragraph, as in our case, or employing other embedding models.

The `information_retrieval_and_rag_gemini.ipynb` notebook contains the code for this example and the `information_retrieval_and_rag_gemini.html` file contains the LLM-generated description. The code consists of the following main sections: (1) importing of libraries and defining global variables, including the path to the file with social media posts, and the models to generate the embeddings and the RAG responses; (2) a `get_embeddings_in_batches()` function that generates embeddings for a list of texts by making API calls in batches; (3) a `get_query_embedding()` function that generates an embedding for the user's query; (4) a `retrieve_similar_entries()` function that identifies and returns the entries in a data frame that are the most semantically similar to a given user's query; (5) a `generate_RAG_answer()` function that orchestrates the RAG process; and (6) the main execution block that initializes a Gemini API client, loads the data, and then performs an IR search and a RAG search. As in the previous chapter, the code for the IR and RAG systems is divided into sections to facilitate the explanation.

The following code contains section 1: importing libraries and defining global variables, including the path to the file with social media posts, and the models used to generate the embeddings and the RAG responses.

```
1:      # Import libraries
2:      import os
3:      import pandas as pd
4:      import time
5:
6:      from dotenv import load_dotenv
7:      from google import genai
8:      from google.genai import types
9:      from sklearn.metrics.pairwise import cosine_
        similarity
10:     from IPython.display import display
11:
12:     # Set pandas option to display full text of posts
        in DataFrame
```

(continued)

(continued)

13:	`pd.set_option("display.max_colwidth",` **`None`**`)`
14:	`# Set pandas option to display all rows in DataFrame`
15:	`pd.set_option('display.max_rows',` **`None`**`)`
16:	
17:	`# File paths`
18:	`parquet_path = "../data/All_Synthetic_Data_with_embeddings.parquet"`
19:	`csv_path = "../data/All_Synthetic_Data.csv"`
20:	
21:	`embedding_model = "models/text-embedding-004"`
22:	`rag_generating_model = "gemini-2.5-flash"`
23:	`# Batch size for embedding generation`
24:	`batch_size = 100`

Lines 18 and 19 define a variable containing the relative paths of the files containing the social media posts. The `csv_path` variable contains the path to the file with the posts in comma-separated values (CSV) format. This is the file that we have used throughout the book. The `parquet_path` variable contains the path to the file containing the posts for which embeddings have been generated. Lines 21 and 22 define the models used to generate embeddings and responses to questions. These two tasks require different models.

Line 24 defines a variable `batch_size`. This limits the number of text items sent to the model for embedding creation. We use this batching approach since the number of items to embed can be as large as needed by the users, whereas the quantity that the model can process at a time through the API can be limited. This allows customization of the code for different needs. In this case, we use a batch size of 100.

The following part of the code contains sections 2, 3, and 4: implementation of the `get_embeddings_in_batches()` function, which generates embeddings for a list of texts; the `get_query_embedding()` function, which generates an embedding for a user's query; and the `retrieve_similar_entries()` function, which identifies and returns the entries in a data frame that are the most semantically similar to a given user's query.

```
26:    def get_embeddings_in_batches(texts, model_name,
       batch_size):
27:        """
28:        Generates embeddings for a list of texts in
       batches.
29:
30:        :param texts: A list of strings to embed.
31:        :param model_name: Name of the embedding model to
       use.
32:        :param batch_size: Number of texts to process in
       each API call.
33:        :returns: A list of embeddings.
34:        """
35:        all_embeddings = []
36:        num_batches = (len(texts) + batch_size - 1) //
       batch_size
37:        for i in range(0, len(texts), batch_size):
38:            batch_texts = texts[i: i + batch_size]
39:            display(
40:                f"Processing batch {i//batch_size + 1}/
       {num_batches} "
41:                f"(texts {i+1} to {min(i+batch_size,
       len(texts))})..."
42:            )
43:
44:            result = client.models.embed_content(
45:                model=model_name,
46:                contents=batch_texts,
47:                config=types.EmbedContentConfig(
48:                    task_type="SEMANTIC_SIMILARITY"
49:                )
50:            )
51:            all_embeddings.extend([e.values for e in
       result.embeddings])
52:            display(f"Batch {i//batch_size + 1} processed
       successfully.")
53:            time.sleep(1)
54:
55:        return all_embeddings
56:
57:
58:    def get_query_embedding(text, embedding_model):
59:        result = client.models.embed_content(
60:            model=embedding_model,
61:            contents=text,
```

(continued)

(continued)

62:	config=types.EmbedContentConfig(
63:	task_type="RETRIEVAL_QUERY"
64:	)
65:	)
66:	**return** result.embeddings[0].values
67:	
68:	
69:	**def** retrieve_similar_entries(df, query_embedding, top_n):
70:	df['similarity'] = df['embedding'].apply(
71:	**lambda** x: cosine_similarity([x], [query_embedding])[0][0]
72:	)
73:	**return** df.nlargest(top_n, "similarity")

Lines 26 to 55 implement the get_embeddings_in_batches() function. The function takes as input the list of texts to embed, the name of the model to use to generate the embeddings, and the batch size. The for loop in line 37 iterates over the list of texts in steps of size batch_size (initialized to 100 in line 24). Lines 44 to 50 make the call to the embedding model, indicating SEMATIC_SIMILARITY as the type of embedding to create. Line 51 extracts the list of embeddings from the API call response and appends it to the all_embeddings list, containing the embeddings for all the texts passed in the texts input parameter.

Lines 58 to 66 define the get_query_embedding() function that computes the embedding for the user's query. Note that the model is instructed to produce a RETRIEVAL_QUERY embedding, which is optimized for information retrieval tasks.

Lines 69 to 73 implement the retrieve_similar_entries() function, which is the core of our information retrieval example. The function first computes the cosine similarity between each post's embedding and the user's query embedding. Then, it assigns the result to a new column in the data frame called "similarity". The function then finds and returns the top_n posts with the highest cosine similarity (the default of top_n is set to 10).

The following part of the code contains section 5: implementation of the generate_RAG_answer() function that orchestrates the RAG process.

```
 76:    def generate_RAG_answer(
 77:        query,
 78:        df_posts,
 79:        top_n=10,
 80:        embedding_model=embedding_model,
 81:        generating_model=rag_generating_model,
 82:        topP=0.8,
 83:        temperature=1.0
 84:    ):
 85:        """
 86:        Generates a RAG answer based on the query and
        semantically
 87:        close posts.
 88:
 89:        :param query: The user's query.
 90:        :param df_posts: DataFrame with posts and their
        embeddings.
 91:        :param top_n: Number of top similar posts to
        consider for
 92:        generating the answer.
 93:        :param embedding_model: Model to use for generating
        embeddings.
 94:        :param generating_model: Model to use for generating
        the answer.
 95:        :param topP: Top-P sampling parameter for
        generation.
 96:        :param temperature: Temperature parameter for
        generation.
 97:        :returns: The generated answer based on the
        retrieved posts.
 98:        """
 99:        query_embedding = get_query_embedding(
100:            query,
101:            embedding_model
102:        )
103:        similar_posts = retrieve_similar_entries(
104:            df_posts,
105:            query_embedding,
106:            top_n
107:        )
108:        display(similar_posts[['owner', 'post_text',
        'similarity']])
109:
110:        # Combine the text of the posts as context for the
        answer
```

(continued)

(continued)

```
111:            context = "\n".join(similar_posts['post_
        text'].values)
112:
113:            # Set the system and user messages to the model
114:            system_message = (
115:                "You are a helpful assistant that provides
        answers "
116:                "based on social media posts."
117:            )
118:            user_message = f"''
119:                Based on the following context, please provide
        an answer
120:                to the query.
121:                Only use the information provided in the context
        to answer
122:                the query.

124:                Context: {context}
125:                Query: {query}
126:            "'
127:
128:            # Retrieve the model's response
129:            result = client.models.generate_content(
130:                model=generating_model,
131:                # https://ai.google.dev/api/generate-content#generationco
        nfig
132:                config=types.GenerateContentConfig(
133:                system_instruction=system_message,
134:                # max cumulative prob of tokens to consider when
        sampling
135:                    topP=topP,
136:                    # Randomness of the output
137:                    # 0.0 = deterministic, 2.0 = most random
138:                    temperature=temperature
139:                ),
140:                contents=user_message
141:            )
142:
143:        return result.text
```

Lines 76 to 143 implement the function. The function takes as inputs the user's query, the data frame with the social media posts, the maximum number top_n of the IR results to return (setting the default to 10), the names of the embedding and text generation models to use, and finally, the `temperature` and `topP` parameters that control the randomness of the output from the text generation model (explained in Chapter 2). The function first generates the embedding for the query and computes the list of posts that are semantically similar to the query. After these results are displayed, the function defines the system and user messages for the model that will generate the response to the user's query. The `context` variable defined in line 111 contains the list of similar posts as a single string, which was processed in lines 103 to 107. Lines 114 to 117 define the `system_message`, and lines 118 to 126 define the `user_message` string. Both the `context` and the user's query are included in this message. Lines 129 to 141 make the API call to the model, including `system_message`, `user_message`, and the `topP` and `temperature` parameters.

The following part of the code contains section 6: implementation of the main execution block that initializes a Gemini API client, loads the data, and then performs an IR search and a RAG search.

```
145:    # Load environment variables and get API key
146:    load_dotenv()
147:    api_key = os.getenv("GEMINI_API_KEY")
148:    if not api_key:
149:        raise ValueError(
150:            "Missing GEMINI_API_KEY in environment or .env
        file"
151:        )
152:    client = genai.Client(api_key=api_key)
153:
154:    # Load social media posts and embeddings
155:    if os.path.exists(parquet_path):
156:        display(f"Loading posts and embeddings from {parquet_
        path}...")
157:        df_posts = pd.read_parquet(parquet_path)
158:    else:
159:        display(f"Loading posts from {csv_path} and generating
        embeddings...")
160:        df_posts = pd.read_csv(csv_path)
161:        docs = df_posts.post_text.tolist()
162:        embeddings = get_embeddings_in_batches(
163:            docs,
164:            embedding_model,
165:            batch_size
166:        )
167:        df_posts["embedding"] = embeddings
```

(continued)

(continued)

```
168:        df_posts.to_parquet(parquet_path, index=False)
169:        display(f"Saved posts with embeddings to {parquet_
            path}.")
170:
171:    # Example #1: Information Retrieval
172:
173:    q= """
174:        Self-promotion highlights
175:        accomplishments and competence
176:    """
177:    query_embedding = get_query_embedding(q, embedding_model)
178:    similarity = retrieve_similar_entries(df_posts, query_
            embedding, 10)
179:
180:    print(q)
181:    display(similarity[['owner', 'post_text', 'similarity']])
```

Lines 145 to 201 contain the main execution block of the code. The first part loads the API key and initializes the client to interact with the Gemini model through its API. The second part, in lines 155 to 169, loads the dataset of social media posts, either from a preprocessed file in parquet format with embeddings or from a raw CSV file, generating embeddings if necessary. Since generating the embeddings can be computationally expensive, the code first checks if the embeddings have been generated in a previous execution of the notebook, and if so, it reads the file containing them. If they have not, the code generates the embeddings and saves them to a file from which the embeddings can be read in the future. The name and format of this file, represented by the parquet_ path variable, are different from those of the original file represented by the csv_path variable. This is a caching technique used to avoid unnecessarily recomputing the embeddings.

Lines 173 to 181 implement a simple IR example. A query is first defined and assigned to a variable named q. Then, the embedding for the query is created with the get_query_embedding() function, and the retrieve_similar_entries() function is called to retrieve the list of up to 10 posts most similar to the query. The outputs of these lines are shown in Fig. 10.1.

	owner	post_text	similarity
	Self-promotion highlights accomplishments and competence		
330	Lady equality	I'm reflecting on the importance of being visi...	0.681246
978	Student-f	Reflecting on my personal growth as a Latina s...	0.666544
239	Lady equality	Celebrating small wins at work today! 🎉 Recent...	0.666211
1094	Student-m	As we approach the end of the semester, I enco...	0.666071
276	Lady equality	Just completed my certification in project man...	0.661739
901	Student-f	Just finished a session on public speaking! It...	0.660177
1003	Student-f	I recently organized an art exhibit highlighti...	0.658711
388	Medical-f	As we wrap up the year, let's reflect on our p...	0.658347
281	Lady equality	Yesterday, I celebrated a little victory at wo...	0.654916
250	Lady equality	Today marks one year since our initiative to b...	0.654143

Fig. 10.1 IR example 1 output using self-promotion as query, from the information_retrieval_and_rag_gemini.ipynb notebook

Finally, lines 185 to 201 show how to use the generate_RAG_ answer() function to implement a single question-and-answer interaction with the dataset. The code is as follows:

```
183:        # Example #2: Retrieval-Augmented Generation (RAG)
184:
185:        query = """
186:            Are there posts in this dataset that use
                impression management
187:            techniques like self-promotion, ingratiation, or
                supplication?
188:        """
189:
190:        answer = generate_RAG_answer(
191:            query,
192:            df_posts,
193:            top_n=10,
194:            embedding_model=embedding_model,
195:            generating_model=rag_generating_model,
196:            topP=0.8,
197:            temperature=1.0
198:        )
```

(continued)

(continued)

```
199:
200:                print(f"Query: {query}")
201:                print(f"Answer: {answer}")
```

Lines 183 to 188 define the user query as a string assigned to the query variable, which is then passed to the generate_RAG_answer() function along with the other parameters. These lines can be changed to interrogate the data with a different query or use different values for the other parameters. The response from the model is assigned to the answer variable. Lines 200 and 201 display the user's query and the response from the model.

The code displays a data frame of the 10 most similar posts, similar to the IR example, and a generated response. For brevity, only the generated response is shown in Fig. 10.2.

Query:

Are there posts in this dataset that use impression management techniques like self-promotion, ingratiation, or supplication?

Answer:

Yes, there are posts that use impression management techniques:

- **Self-promotion:**
  - "Art has a unique power to capture social issues. I recently started a blog to analyze how modern art reflects our current political climate. I invite everyone to join me in this conversation—how does art influence your perception of societal issues?" (The user is promoting their newly started blog.)
- **Supplication:**
  - "As my peers and I prepare for our professional careers, I believe networking is crucial. I welcome any advice or insights from those who have successfully navigated this process. What strategies have you found effective in building professional relationships?" (The user is asking for advice, which is a form of supplication.)

Fig. 10.2 RAG output from a self-promotion query, from the information_retrieval_and_rag_gemini.ipynb notebook

CONSIDERATIONS OF IR AND RAG
FOR QUALITATIVE ANALYSIS

In this section, we address a set of design decisions that affect the outcomes of the IR and RAG systems. These include the text chunking strategy, the chosen model and its parameters, the number of retrieved items, and query crafting. We also discuss the risk of circularity in qualitative analysis that IR and RAG systems can cause.

A first decision is the size of the text chunks since it will be the unit of analysis of the IR or RAG system. Text can be chunked into sentences, paragraphs, pages, or complete documents. In addition, the chunks can overlap to preserve context across chunks or not. Using small chunks results in more specific embeddings than using larger chunks but also results in a larger number of embeddings, which can increase the amount of storage and computation needed. In our example, we decided for simplicity to make each entire social media post a chunk and to have no overlap between chunks. This is because social media posts are generally not as strongly related to each other as paragraphs in an interview transcript or narrative documents such as blog posts and 10-K annual financial reports. Researchers need to choose the chunk size and level of overlap on the basis of the nature of the data and the goals of the analysis.

Another important design decision is the choice of models and their parameter values. In our example, we used two different Google's Gemini models: the gemini-embedding-001 model to create embeddings and the gemini-2.5-flash model to generate text. Currently, these are the latest models available through the Gemini API. They are likely to be superseded by new models over time. Small generic models are generally faster and less expensive than large models but may not fully capture the nuance of domain-specific language, diminishing the retrieval performance. Small models fine-tuned for the specific task at hand are preferable since they deliver the best performance at the lowest possible cost. Due to the generative module of an RAG system and the stochastic nature of LLMs, the responses can vary from one execution to another. As explained in Chapter 2, the level of randomness can be controlled through the values of the temperature or top_p parameters. It is recommended to use one or the other, but not both at the same time. A temperature lower than 1 makes the output more deterministic, and a value higher than 1 makes it more random. The OpenAI and Gemini APIs accept temperature values between 0 and 2. The top-p parameter restricts the set of tokens to select from to those with the highest probability. A low top-p value makes the output more deterministic, and a high value makes it more random. The OpenAI and Gemini APIs accept top-p values greater than 0 and up to 1. In the example above, the temperature was set to the default value of 1. The top-p parameter was set to 0.8, meaning that during text generation, each next token is randomly selected from the subset of tokens with the highest probability, whose cumulative probability is up to 80%.

The number of retrieved items influences the output generated. In the example, we limit the number of items to 10. A larger set of items will provide more context to the LLM, but at the same time, it will include items with lower cosine similarity, which may be less relevant to the query. We recommend experimenting with different values of these parameters to determine what is best suited for your research project.

Query crafting is a critical consideration that requires an iterative process. Query crafting begins with a phase of conceptual exploration, where initial queries are formulated to test preliminary ideas. The outputs of the LLMs are then used to refine the initial ideas iteratively and create more precise and effective queries (Garcia Quevedo et al., 2025).

The benefits of query crafting become more evident when implementing RAG. The generative capabilities of LLMs enable a dynamic question-and-answer system that supports a deeper exploration and understanding of the data. The query used in the sample code above illustrates the use of RAG merging information retrieval and text generation.

To exemplify query crafting, we continue to use the theoretical framework of impression management and the dataset of synthetic social media posts used in previous chapters. Initial queries can be created via the theoretical framework or the research aims. The code explained in the previous section uses the following query: "Self-promotion highlights accomplishments and competence" to find posts that express self-promotion. The highest similarity score for this query is 0.681. This initial query can be further refined by introducing more context. For example, the following query uses the previous definition and more context: "Self-promotion highlights accomplishments and competency like the following: Excited to announce my company's new initiative." For this last query, the highest similarity score is 0.759 (the output of this execution is not shown for brevity reasons). However, most of the retrieved posts refer to posts about the company's achievements. Query crafting is an iterative process of query refinement that helps researchers clarify their interpretations and intent.

RAG is a versatile tool that allows researchers to explore data deeply, challenge preliminary ideas, and refine interpretations. We encourage researchers to experiment with different models for embedding creation and text generation, model parameters (e.g., temperature and top-p), number of posts retrieved, and queries, since the results are sensitive to variations in these inputs.

IR and RAG enable deeper interaction with the data, allowing for more nuanced inquiries during the analytical process. They enable the connection between the data and the theoretical framework, research questions, and researcher objectives. This means that, through the system inputs, the researcher must make their research intentions and theoretical paradigms evident. Through this conscious process of inquiring about the dataset, the researcher can improve their own reflection and analytical process.

In addition to important technical choices when implementing IR and RAG, a crucial consideration when using them is the risk of circularity, which refers to the researcher's confirmatory bias, particularly during data analysis (Dana & Dumez, 2015). As information retrieval and RAG are guided by the researcher's assumptions and interpretations, these may unintentionally lead to queries and questions that reinforce their initial explanations. Garcia Quevedo et al. (2025) caution researchers against using IR alone and instead propose its use in combination with classification and clustering tasks as a way to triangulate and deepen their analysis.

LLMs are evolving constantly. New models process text, images, sounds, and videos in combination, offering extensive customization. In the final chapter, we explore possibilities that can also be used to expand the toolbox for qualitative analysis.

References

Dana, L. P., & Dumez, H. (2015). Qualitative research revisited: Epistemology of a comprehensive approach. *International Journal of Entrepreneurship and Small Business, 26*(2), 154–170. https://doi.org/10.1504/IJESB.2015.071822

Garcia Quevedo, D., Glaser, A., & Verzat, C. (2025). Enhancing theorization using artificial intelligence: Leveraging large language models for qualitative analysis of online data. *Organizational Research Methods 29*(1), 92–112. https://doi.org/10.1177/10944281251339144

Jurafsky, D., & Martin, J. H. (2025). *Speech and language processing: An introduction to natural language processing, computational linguistics, and speech recognition, with language models* (3rd ed.). Online manuscript released August 24, 2025. https://web.stanford.edu/~jurafsky/slp3/

Simon, S., Mailach, A., Dorn, J., & Siegmund, N. (2024). *A methodology for evaluating RAG systems: A case study on configuration dependency validation* (No. arXiv:2410.08801). arXiv. https://doi.org/10.48550/arXiv.2410.08801

Spielberger, G., Artinger, F., Reb, J., & Kerschreiter, R. (2025). *Retrieval augmented generation for topic modeling in organizational research: An introduction with empirical demonstration* (No. arXiv:2502.20963). arXiv. https://doi.org/10.48550/arXiv.2502.20963

CHAPTER 11

Perspectives on LLMs in Management and Qualitative Research

Abstract This chapter explores the evolving role of large language models (LLMs) in management and qualitative research, considering their transformative impact on research. It discusses the transition from basic text analysis tools to sophisticated analytical assistants, propelled by advancements in multimodal models, reasoning models, and agentic AI. Future developments are envisioned, such as LLMs processing various data formats and supporting complex reasoning tasks, enabling researchers to automate labor-intensive workflows. The chapter concludes by encouraging researchers to critically engage with AI technologies, striking a balance between the benefits of AI-driven insights and the need to mitigate their limitations.

Keywords Multimodal models · Agentic AI · Reasoning models

In the preceding chapters, we navigated the evolving landscape of AI in management and qualitative research. We have seen how tools like large language models are no longer a novelty but a fundamental capability, streamlining the analysis of vast text datasets at unprecedented speed. Techniques such as classification, topic modeling, and information retrieval have empowered researchers to efficiently identify themes, sentiments, and patterns across thousands of data points, transforming what was once a laborious process into a dynamic and scalable workflow.

D. Garcia Quevedo and J. Kuri, *AI for Qualitative Research*,
https://doi.org/10.1007/978-3-032-08872-7_11

This book, however, has focused not only on what LLMs are but also on how these models work and why it is important for researchers to understand and use them. We have strived to cultivate a critical understanding of LLMs' capabilities and potential pitfalls, fostering the development of best practices that safeguard the integrity and validity of research. It is our hope that by doing so, we have contributed to the ongoing collective effort to ensure that AI, when thoughtfully and knowledgeably integrated into the research process, serves to advance both knowledge and society.

While the benefits we have discussed are significant, they represent only the beginning of a broader transition. The emerging frontier of AI in research is characterized by a shift from simple text analysis tools to substantive analytical assistants. This transformation will be driven by four key developments, each poised to redefine the research lifecycle: multimodal models, reasoning models, agentic AI systems, and deep research capabilities.

The Advent of Multimodal Analysis

To date, the application of LLMs has been predominantly limited to text. However, the future will see multimodal models overcome this limitation by natively processing information in text, image, audio, and video formats (Yin et al., 2024). This capability will allow researchers to capture the rich contextual data often lost in text-only analysis. For example, a multimodal model could analyze a video recording of a meeting, correlating spoken sentiment with vocal tone and nonverbal cues to identify moments of incongruence, such as a confident statement contradicted by hesitant body language. Similarly, in an ethnographic study, a researcher could supplement field notes with photographs of an office environment, analyzed to understand how architectural features influence social dynamics and collaboration.

The Power of Reasoning Models

Current LLMs, while powerful, have a limited capacity for complex reasoning. This is changing with new reasoning models designed for multistep logical analysis. These models can deconstruct complex problems, formulate hypotheses, and critique the logical consistency of arguments (Wei et al., 2022). For qualitative researchers, this introduces new avenues for automated grounded theory development. For example, a reasoning model could be prompted with hundreds of in-depth interviews on employee burnout to develop a theoretical framework, outlining antecedent conditions, core phenomena, and causal links. This approach leverages AI not only for data coding but also as a genuine partner in the sense-making process of theory building.

AUTOMATION WITH AGENTIC AI

Perhaps the most significant paradigm shift will emerge from the rise of agentic AI. In contrast to current models that react to discrete prompts, an AI agent is an autonomous system capable of comprehending a high-level objective, decomposing it into subtasks, and executing a multistep plan (Shenson, 2025). This signifies the arrival of a functional digital research assistant, capable of automating the most laborious and time-consuming aspects of the research workflow.

Consider a researcher studying the public reaction to a company's sustainability initiative. Instead of spending hours gathering data, the researcher could give an AI agent a single, high-level directive: "Produce a comprehensive report on the stakeholder response." The agent would then independently formulate and execute a plan, gathering press releases, social media data, and news articles; performing sentiment and thematic analysis; and synthesizing all findings into a structured report. The researcher is consequently liberated from preliminary analysis and empowered to focus on interpreting the findings and crafting the final narrative.

SYNTHESIZING KNOWLEDGE WITH DEEP RESEARCH

A specialized and potent application of agentic AI is the emerging capability of deep research. Whereas a standard web search returns a list of hyperlinks, a deep research agent synthesizes information from hundreds of sources to produce a single, comprehensive, and cited report. This capability is a significant catalyst for overcoming one of the primary impediments in the academic workflow: the literature review. A doctoral student can prompt a deep research tool to conduct a thorough literature review on a new topic. Within minutes, the AI tool can deliver a multipage document that would have traditionally required weeks or months to compile, providing a robust foundation from which the student can initiate their original scholarly contribution.

Final Words

The advancements in multimodal, reasoning, and agentic AI promise a future where the researcher's role focuses on strategic thinking, critical evaluation, and creative synthesis, rather than on data collection and processing. However, this future also comes with risks and limitations that we are still in the early stages of comprehending. Our final message is this: by remaining knowledgeable of the technology and maintaining a critical position on these new advances, we can take advantage of these developments while mitigating their risks. The future of research is not settled, and we must be prepared to shape its course.

References

Shenson, J. (2025, April 25). *Agentic artificial intelligence: Evolution, core capabilities, and challenges.* IEEE Computer Society. https://www.computer.org/publications/tech-news/trends/agentic-ai/

Wei, J., Wang, X., Schuurmans, D., Bosma, M., Ichter, B., Xia, F., Chi, E. H., Le, Q. V., & Zhou, D. (2022). Chain-of-thought prompting elicits reasoning in large language models. *36th Conference on Neural Information Processing Systems,* 24824–24837.

Yin, S., Fu, C., Zhao, S., Li, K., Sun, X., Xu, T., & Chen, E. (2024). A survey on multimodal large language models. *National Science Review, 11*(12), nwae403. https://doi.org/10.1093/nsr/nwae403

INDEX

© The Editor(s) (if applicable) and The Author(s) 2026
D. Garcia Quevedo and J. Kuri, *AI for Qualitative Research*,
https://doi.org/10.1007/978-3-032-08872-7

If you have any concerns about our products,
you can contact us on
ProductSafety@springernature.com

In case Publisher is established outside the EU,
the EU authorized representative is:
**Springer Nature Customer Service Center GmbH
Europaplatz 3, 69115 Heidelberg, Germany**

Printed by Libri Plureos GmbH
in Hamburg, Germany